T0324767

SPRINGER SERIES
IN PERCEPTION ENGINEERING

Series Editor: Ramesh Jain

Springer Series
In Perception Engineering

Ting-Jun Fan

Describing and Recognizing 3-D Objects Using Surface Properties

With 68 Illustrations

Springer-Verlag
New York Berlin Heidelberg
London Paris Tokyo Hong Kong

Ting-Jun Fan
IBM T.J. Watson Research Center
Yorktown Heights, NY 10598
USA

Series Editor
Ramesh Jain
Electrical Engineering
  and Computer Science Department
The University of Michigan
Ann Arbor, MI 48109
USA

Library of Congress Cataloging-in-Publication Data
Fan, Ting-Jun.
    Describing and recognizing 3-D objects using surface properties /
Ting-Jun Fan.—(Springer series in perception engineering)
        p. cm.—(Springer series in perception engineering)
    Includes bibliographical references.
    1. Image processing. 2. Surfaces (Technology) I. Title.
II. Series.
TA1632.F36 1990
006.4′2—dc20   89-21848

Camera-ready text prepared by the author using LaTeX.
Printed and bound by Edwards Brothers, Inc., Ann Arbor, Michigan.
Printed in the United States of America.

9 8 7 6 5 4 3 2 1

ISBN 0-387-97179-3 Springer-Verlag New York Berlin Heidelberg
ISBN 3-540-97179-3 Springer-Verlag Berlin Heidelberg New York

Preface

Surface properties play a very important role in many perception tasks. Object recognition, navigation, and inspection use surface properties extensively. Characterizing surfaces at different scales in given data is often the first and possibly the most important step. Most early research in machine perception relied on only very coarse characterization of surfaces. In the last few years, surface characterization has been receiving due attention.

Dr. T. J. Fan is one of the very few researchers who designed and implemented a complete system for object recognition. He studied issues related to characterization of surfaces in the context of object recognition, and then uses the features thus developed for recognizing objects. He uses a multi-view representation of 3-D objects for recognition, and he develops techniques for the segmentation of range images to obtain features for recognition. His matching approach also allows him to recognize objects from their partial views in the presence of other occluding objects. The efficacy of his approach is demonstrated in many examples.

Since the emphasis in this work is on surface characterization, range images offer an excellent domain to study issues without trivializing the problem and without any unnecessary complexity. Range images have become increasing in popular due to the above and to the fact that techniques for acquiring and processing range images are now making them applicable to many industrial problems. Fan's book is the third book in the Springer Series in Perception Engineering on this topic. Besl's book addresses surface characterization and segmentation, the book by Jain and Jain gives an overview of the field in collected articles from several experts, and now, T. J. Fan describes a complete system for object recognition.

Ramesh Jain
Ann Arbor, Michigan

Contents

List of Tables

List of Figures

xii   List of Figures

1

Introduction

Computer vision has been a very active and productive research field for the past two decades. Its goal is to allow a machine to understand its environment and perform required tasks using perceptual information. It also has direct application in areas such as character recognition, motion analysis, medical diagnosis, and remote sensing. The recognition of 3-D objects is a central problem in the field of computer vision. It is a necessary step in many industrial applications, such as the identification of industrial parts, the automation of the manufacturing processes, and offers the hope for more intelligent robots who will be equipped with a powerful visual feedback system.

3-D object recognition consists of identifying an object in a scene with a model, so that the correspondences between the object and the model is established, and the 3-D information, such as the orientation and position of the object, is obtained.

Two major factors condition the performance and competence of a recognition system. One is the method used to describe the objects and models, the other is the method used to establish the correspondences between objects and models. These issues can be summarized as follows:

- *Description* — How do we represent the 3-D objects? What *features* should be extracted from a scene (originally viewer centered) in order to describe physical properties of objects and their spatial inter-relationships?

- *Matching* — How do we establish the correspondences between scene features and object models in order to recognize objects in a complex scene?

The purpose of the research presented in this book is to provide satisfying solutions to the above issues by developing a complete system which automatically describes 3-D objects, uses the same descriptions to represent model and scene objects, and recognizes each scene object by identifying it with one of the models. We also contrast our approach to previous work in the domain [32,33,34] and present successful results on a variety of complex objects in scenes with multiple objects occluding each other.

In this chapter, we begin by discussing the input used in our system, then present our criteria for choosing a shape description mechanism, discuss the issues in object recognition, list the detailed problems of the research, summarize the main contribution of the research, and finally outline the remainder of this book.

1.1   The Input

Intensity images are used as the primary input in most of the computer vision studies. However, in 3-D scene analysis, these images introduce difficulties in interpreting features. For example, an edge which introduces a discontinuity in intensity images may not correspond to a true discontinuity in 3-D; it can be due to shadow, surface marking, or illumination. Further reasoning is needed to infer 3-D information from intensity features, unfortunately, this is a very difficult problem far from being solved at this time.

Since the 1970s, *range images* which contain direct 3-D properties of objects have been available. Each pixel of the image represents a *depth* value of the object surface, which represents a relative distance between the surface point and the viewer. Using range images, the ambiguities of the feature interpretation mentioned above are eliminated. In this book, it is assumed that range data of the points on the visible surfaces are available, for example, by the use of a laser range finder [53,84]. It is also assumed that these data are *dense*, in the sense of being sampled on a certain grid and not just at discontinuities, as may be the case for uninterpreted edge-based stereo data.

1.2   Issues in Shape Description

1.2.1   CRITERIA FOR SHAPE DESCRIPTION

In order to retrieve significant information from scenes of 3-D objects and effectively represent these objects, a good description method is needed. We believe that it should satisfy the following criteria:

- *richness* — The description should capture enough information about each object such that similar objects can be identified. It should also enable us to recreate, from it, a shape reasonably close to the original object.

- *stability* — Local changes due to noise and digitization errors should not radically alter the description. Since such changes are not avoidable, it is very important that the description be stable with respect to these changes.

- *local support* — Partially visible objects must still be identified. Occlusion always exists in scenes of 3-D objects, to identify similar objects and correctly recognize the appropriate object, the description should be robust to occlusion.

- *naturalness* — The description should correspond to physical features. Physical features such as surface edges are more stable in envi-

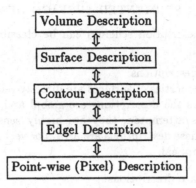

FIGURE 1.1. Levels of descriptions.

ronment changes, as opposed to those features forced by an arbitrary approximating scheme.

- *reliability* — The computation should be robust in the sense that only a reasonable amount of error is generated during the computation process.

- *efficiency* — The computation must only require a reasonable amount of time and space.

Unfortunately, some of the above criteria are mutually exclusive. For example, the richer the description, the more computation it will need, thus reducing the efficiency of the description.

Objects can be described at different levels as shown in Figure 1.1. Lower level descriptions such as point-wise and edgel descriptions are easier to compute. For example, a range array may be available directly as input and an Extended Gaussian Image [45] requires only the computation of surface normals. However, these lower levels are not stable with respect to viewing directions and not very tolerant to occlusion. Higher level descriptions, on the other hand, maintain their invariance with respect to the change of environments, but the algorithms to compute them are very expensive. For example, volume descriptions are very high level, however, techniques for computing them are not yet fully developed. Currently, the objects used in volume descriptions are restricted to mostly simple and regular shapes [74].

In summary, the description should be chosen at a level as high as possible while being robust and efficient. From the above discussion, we found that a description in terms of visible surface properties is a good candidate. Surface descriptions are richer than edge and pixel descriptions; furthermore, the computation of surface description is much more robust than that of volume descriptions.

1.2.2 CHOOSING SEGMENTED SURFACE DESCRIPTIONS

In general, surface description schemes can be classified into two major classes as follows:

- *Global* surface descriptions:
  In this class, properties of surfaces are directly retrieved from images [45,54,56,81]. As the descriptions are global and no explicit surface segmentation is attempted, they are highly sensitive to occlusion. Furthermore, these descriptions are arrays or vectors of numbers with little intuitive appeal.

- *Segmented* surface descriptions:
  In this class, the visible surfaces of objects are first segmented into surface *patches*, and the information about surfaces is computed from these patches. Since these descriptions consist of *combinations* of smaller patch descriptions, they are in general less sensitive to occlusion than the previous ones. Descriptions in this class can be further classified as follows:

  - Approximation by *simple* surfaces:
    In this category, surfaces are approximated by planar or simple shaped patches [13,23,42,43,61,66]. Such methods generally do not attempt to find significant surface features prior to approximation, rather, the surface is segmented arbitrarily whenever the fit is not satisfactory. We believe that such methods are rather poor for computer vision, as the approximating surfaces are subject to large changes even if the observed surfaces change only slightly. Furthermore, the number of patches found could be typically very large and the points and lines where the approximating patches are joined need not have any *physical* significance.

  - Segmented surface descriptions:
    In this category, surfaces of range images are segmented at *physical* significant features, such as *discontinuities* of these surfaces [8,23,55]. These descriptions are better than the previous ones in the sense that they are more stable with respect to small changes on the observed surfaces, and usually contain a lower number of patches. However, most of the existing methods do not lead to a complete segmentation [23,55], while others require a rather complex control structure [8].

From the above discussion, we conclude that segmented surface descriptions at physical features are the best choice for our purpose. In this book, discontinuities such as *jump boundaries*, *limbs*, and *creases* are chosen to segment surfaces since they are the most explicit features on surfaces of 3-D objects.

1.3 Issues of Recognition

Recognizing objects is one of the major tasks in computer vision. In general, two steps are involved: *building models* and *recognizing scene objects*. We think that a good recognition system should provide the following:

- It should automatically build object models from range images.

- The descriptions used for models and for scenes of unknown objects should be compatible, or at least it should be easy to go from one to the other.

- The search should be efficient in finding correspondences between models and scene objects.

1.3.1 DESCRIPTION OF MODELS

Methods in representing 3-D object models can be classified as follows (more details are given in Chapter 2).

- Specific features:
  In this class, object models are represented by specific features [2,17]. Such models usually contain very few features, such as the distance between two significant points, and those features mainly describe the *differences* among models. Each unknown object is recognized as one of the models by detecting those significant features in that model. Such model representations usually require the full study of model objects before deciding which features should be used, and usually need very sophisticated modeling systems. The selection of which features are sufficient to discriminate adequately among objects is determined by trial and error. Therefore, modifications are required for the original model features when new models are included, hence flexibility is highly restricted.

- 2-D or $2\frac{1}{2}$D representation with one view:
  In this class, only a particular view of the model objects is represented [24,67], and views from other directions are completely ignored, hence they impose severe restrictions on the amount of changes in the viewing directions.

- 3-D representation:
  In this class, highly organized 3-D object descriptions are used for the models [25]. The main advantage of this class of representations is that it provides an exact description that is object centered. The main disadvantage is that it is necessary to perform translation in matching 3-D models and 2-D observed images, and this translation is always very expensive. Furthermore, it is very difficult to obtain such

a 3-D model representation automatically, either from range images or other sensory sources, therefore the models are always manually built.

- Multi-view representation:
  In this class, each 3-D object model is represented by multiple 2D or $2\frac{1}{2}$D descriptions, each of which represents one particular view of this model [38,50]. The advantages of these methods are as follows:

  - Generating such model descriptions is easier compared to 3-D representations.
  - Since representations of scene objects can be obtained in a similar way, the descriptions for model and scene objects can then be compatible.
  - They contain more information than 2-D representations.
  - The methods used here can be *data-driven*, i.e., no a priori knowledge about the scene objects is required. This is more flexible than those methods using specific feature representations in which modifications are required for the original model features when new models are included.

  However, current methods suffer from a common problem that the number of views is generally large, which significantly reduces the efficiency and increases the space of the system.

In order to build object models automatically and to maintain compatible descriptions for both model and scene objects, we have decided to use *multi-view* models. Furthermore, to save space and enhance efficiency, each model consists of only 2 to 6 views. These views are arranged such that most of the significant surfaces of the model object are contained in at least one of the views. The same description method is used to describe model views and scene images. Scene objects are identified by matching their descriptions to those of the model views.

1.3.2 MATCHING PRIMITIVES AND ALGORITHMS

The efficiency and robustness of a recognition system is crucially dependent on the primitives and algorithms used in the matching process. We have decided to use *segmented surface* descriptions in our research; however, the primitives of the descriptions can vary. They can be pure equations of surface patches, or more compact symbolic representations. In terms of segmented surface descriptions, we think good primitives should contain the following characteristics:

- They should be *symbolic*, since symbolic representations are compact and easy to represent the properties of surface features, such as the type of their boundaries.

- Although we are dealing with $2\frac{1}{2}$D images, it is still possible to retrieve information in terms of the coordinates of the objects, rather than those of the viewer. Such primitives, which are *object-centered*, are less sensitive to changes in viewing direction and occlusion.

- They should not only contain information about the segmented surface patches, but also about the relationships between these surface patches.

On the other hand, we think that a good algorithm should satisfy the following criteria:

- The algorithm should be flexible, that is, it should allow variations in descriptions. A small change in description should not affect the result of matching, as is the case in subgraph isomorphism.

- The search should be efficient.

- Geometric information should be used to verify the matching. The main advantage of using geometric information is that it allows direct comparisons between image data and models and its matching criteria are usually clear.

In this book, we have decided to use *attributed graphs*, or *graphs*, as the primitives of our system. Descriptions of 3-D surfaces are represented by graphs whose *nodes* contain the information about the surface patches and *links* the relationships between surface patches. Furthermore, a *graph matching* algorithm, which uses the *geometrical constraints*, is selected for our recognition system. In general, such a choice satisfies the above criterion.

1.4   Questions for the Research

The above discussion summarizes the goals and inputs for what is attempted in the research. In this section, we summarize the key questions that are evoked throughout this book:

1. Description of scene:

   - What are appropriate criteria for shape description?
   - How to perform the computation of the chosen description?
   - How are the descriptions affected by factors such as noise, occlusion, and viewing directions?
   - What are the limits of the chosen descriptors?
   - How can this description be used?

2. Recognition:

- How to build the models for recognition?
- What matching algorithm should be chosen?
- How to evaluate the assumptions?
- What is the performance in terms of efficiency and robustness?

3. Results:

- How to evaluate the results of the research?

In the remainder of this document, we will try to provide answers to the above questions, explicitly or implicitly. However, the results shown in this book should not be viewed as final solutions to the above questions, instead, they should be viewed as a step which leads to better image understanding.

1.5   The Contribution of the Research

The main goal of the research presented here is to provide a method to describe and recognize 3-D objects, using the surface information of these objects. The main achievements are:

- It provides a *full* system, starting from a range image of a scene, to describe and recognize the 3-D objects in it. This includes detecting surface features, segmenting and describing surfaces of objects, using the same descriptions as multi-view models, and recognizing scene objects.

- The description computation is data-driven, i.e., no a priori knowledge about the model and scene objects is required.

- The matching process is tolerant to occlusion.

- It successfully describes and recognizes moderately complex objects.

1.6   Organization of the Book

- Chapter 2 presents surveys of existing 3-D object description methods and recognition systems.

- Chapter 3 presents the surface segmentation and description methods, which includes how we go from a dense range map to a set of surface patches, and how these patches are further organized into partial objects.

- Chapter 4 presents the recognition method, which uses the descriptions given above. In the recognition system, matching between all the objects in a scene and the database of all views of all the models is performed by three modules: the *screener*, in which we find the most likely candidate views for each object, the *graph matcher*, which performs a detailed comparison between the potential matching graphs and computes the 3-D transformation between them, and the *analyzer*, which takes a critical look at the results and proposes to split or merge object graphs.

- Chapter 5 presents the experimental results, which include a detailed study on one of our test scenes, the recognition results between 10 model objects and 9 complex scenes, and the experimental results on parallel screening, missing model objects, evaluation on geometric transform, and the performance of our recognition system under occlusion.

- Chapter 6 offers discussions, conclusions, and ideas for future research.

2

Survey of Previous Work

Shape description plays an important role in the research area of object recognition. A large number of methods have been proposed to solve the problem of recognizing objects based on different descriptions such as volumes, surfaces, and curves. In this chapter, we provide a survey on different shape description methods, and also survey relevant work dealing with object recognition. We do not aim for a complete survey here, Besl and Jain [9] and Chin [28] provide excellent overviews of the fields of range image analysis and object recognition. Nevatia [65] and Ballard and Brown [6] offer surveys on descriptions and recognition systems whose inputs are not restricted to range images.

In the first section of this chapter, alternative methods for shape description are discussed. In the second section, existing object recognition systems are listed, their advantages and disadvantages are also discussed.

2.1 Survey of Shape Descriptions

3-D objects in range images can be described in terms of their 2-D projections [15]. However, such descriptions are highly dependent on the viewing directions and do not contain information about the 3-D shape of the objects. Therefore, we are interested in 3-D shape descriptions only. Methods to describe range images of 3-D objects can be classified into the following categories:

- *Volume descriptions* describe an object in terms of solids, such as generalized cylinders, cubes, and blocks.

- *Surface descriptions* describe an object in terms of surfaces or surface patches.

- *Curve/Line descriptions* describe an object in terms of curve and/or line primitives. These primitives usually capture significant features of a surface or among surfaces such as boundary lines of surface discontinuity.

2.1.1 VOLUME DESCRIPTIONS

Cell decomposition

In this class, objects are represented by *quasi-disjoint* cells (they do not share volumes). These cells are usually blocks of relatively small size [6]. Two useful cell decompositions are the oct-tree [51] and kd-tree [7]. This description is easy to compute; however, since the cells are not segmented at *physical* features such as the intersecting plane between two paralleloids, it is not amendable to reasoning, and the number of cells used can be very large even for simple objects.

Generalized cylinders

Generalized cylinders were proposed by Binford as useful volume descriptions for 3-D objects [14]. A generalized cylinder (or generalized cone) is defined as an arbitrary planar shape called a *cross-section*, swept along an arbitrary 3-D curve called an *axis*. In general, the size and the shape of the cross-section may change along the axis, and the rule describing the change is called the *sweep rule* or the *cross-section function*.

Agin [1] obtains generalized cylinder descriptions from range images by first estimating the orientation and position of the axis and fitting circles in planes perpendicular to the axis. The shape described is restricted since only circular cross-sections are used.

Nevatia and Binford [64] compute 3-D cylinders from the 3-D boundaries of objects. In this approach, local cylinders with straight axes are computed and then extended by allowing smooth curving of the axes, and preferred cylinders are selected among various alternatives. The objects are finally described using the properties of the cylinders and their connectivity. The description is also used to recognize objects, which is presented later in detail.

Rao [75,76,77] obtains volumetric shape descriptions from sparse and imperfect data, using generalized cylinders. His system generates descriptions of complex generalized cylinders and compound objects from edges in intensity and range images. The system has been used for grasping application [78].

Shafer [82] and Ponce [73] studied the geometric properties about *straight homogeneous generalized cylinders* (SHGC). No experimental results are given for real images.

Other works related to generalized cylinders can be found in [25,59].

In summary, generalized cylinders are suitable for those objects with *elongated* shapes, but not for other shapes such as terrain maps and polyhedral objects.

Superquadrics

Pentland [70], Bajcsy and Solina [5] and Boult and Gross [19] use superquadrics to represent 3-D objects. The modeling primitive may be thought of as a "lump of clay", which may be deformed and shaped, and is intended to correspond to the notion of a part. However, segmenting complex 3-D objects using superquadrics may be very difficult.

Summary

In general, volumetric descriptions are difficult to compute (except for cell decomposition) and the techniques for computing them are not yet fully developed. Currently, the objects used in volume descriptions are restricted to mostly simple and regular shapes.

2.1.2   CURVE/LINE DESCRIPTIONS

In this category, objects are described in terms of *significant* curves, which usually correspond to object contours or surface discontinuities. The description can be further applied to recognize objects by identifying and comparing such significant curves.

Object contours

Smith and Kanade [83] extract surface contours from range images. These contours can be classified into eight types, each with different characteristics in occluding vs. occluded and different camera/illuminator relationships. In this process, only objects consisting of conical and cylindrical surfaces are used. The extracted contours are further used to predict surface types and build primitives for further recognition, using coherent relationships such as symmetry, collinearity, and being coaxial.

Discontinuities

The jump boundaries in range data can be located easily by rather simple edge operators [31]. The more difficult problem is the detection of other edges such as the ones occurring at creases. Successful methods have been developed for detecting these features when they can be modeled as the intersection of two planar patches [48,62], or when it is reasonable to hypothesize the presence of known objects in the scene [18].

Langridge [55] gives the result of a preliminary investigation into the problem of detecting and locating discontinuities in the first derivatives of surfaces. Results are shown only on two simple synthetic examples.

Nackman [63] proposed to extract *peaks* (local maxima), *pits* (local minima) and *passes* (saddle points) of a surface, to connect these features and obtain a graph which appears useful to describe smooth variations on a surface.

Ponce and Brady [23,72] use surface curvature properties to detect significant boundaries and use a multi-scale approach [85] to locate these features. Boundaries such as surface discontinuities and surface orientation discontinuities are detected. These boundaries can also be applied to compute surface descriptions. This method suffers from large number of iterations and is unstable around surface discontinuities.

Summary

The curve/line descriptions, though relatively easier to compute than volume descriptions, usually contain less information than is necessary to fully describe 3-D objects.

2.1.3 SURFACE DESCRIPTIONS

In our view, methods for 3-D surface descriptions can be classified into two categories:

- *Global* surface descriptions: Properties of surfaces are directly retrieved from images.

- *Segmented* surface descriptions: Surfaces are segmented into surface *patches*. They can be further classified as follows, depending whether they are:

  - approximated by *simple* surfaces, or
  - segmented at *physical* features.

These classes are described below.

Global surface descriptions

The idea of an Extended Gaussian Image (EGI) was introduced by Horn and Ikeuchi [45,46]. The depth maps or needle maps (surface-normal direction maps) computed for real-world scenes are processed to create an orientation histogram for the visible half of the Gaussian sphere for presegmented objects. A very interesting property is that the EGI is unique for convex objects. Furthermore, typical surfaces can be classified using EGI maps. For example, the EGIs of a sphere, a plane, a cone are a sphere, a point, and a small circle, respectively. However, this system is perfect only for convex objects without occlusion, and it can not distinguish among certain shapes as noted in [9].

Sethi and Jayaramamurthy [81] presented an approach for the classification of different types of surfaces in a scene. The surface normal at each point of the surface is computed first, then *characteristic contours* are extracted, which are sets of points for which surface normals are at a constrained inclination with a reference vector. Underlying surfaces are then identified by taking a Hough transform of these contours. This approach works well for simple surfaces such as spheres, cylinders, and cones.

Laffey, Haralick and Watson [54] fit at each pixel a two dimensional cubic polynomial to estimate the first and second partial derivatives at that point. They then compute features to classify each pixel into classes such as peaks or ridges. The output is still a dense representation on which feature extraction has to be performed.

Lin and Perry [56] argued that integrals of the scalar curvature of a 2-D surface of a 3-D object provide easily computed shape information about the object. The computation of these quantities is done using surface triangulation. No experimental results are given in their paper.

We believe that all of these methods suffer from some common deficiencies: As the descriptions are global and no explicit surface segmentation is attempted, they are highly sensitive to occlusion. Also, the descriptions are arrays or vectors of numbers with little intuitive appeal.

Approximation by simple surfaces

Surface representation has been an important area in computer graphics almost from the start. The earliest approaches used approximation by planar patches (typically triangular); later methods have used other surface patches such as *Coons patches* [29] and 2-D splines [69]. Such methods generally do not attempt to find significant surface features prior to approximation, rather, the surface is segmented arbitrarily when the fit is not satisfactory. We believe that such methods, while adequate for graphics applications, are rather poor for computer vision, as the approximating surfaces are subject to large changes even if the observed surfaces change only slightly. As a result, the number of patches found is typically very large and the points and lines where the approximating patches are joined need not have any *physical* significance.

Some examples of using surface approximations for computer vision applications can be found in [13,23,42,43,61,66].

Segmented descriptions

In this category, surfaces of range images are segmented into several patches, then description is based on those segmented surface patches and their relationships.

Besl and Jain [8,10,11,12] presented an algorithm that simultaneously segments a large class of images into regions of arbitrary shape and approximates image data with bivariate functions. In this process, the sign of the Gaussian and mean surface curvatures is used to provide an initial coarse image segmentation into eight fundamental surface types. The segmentation is then refined by an iterative region growing method based on variable-order surface fitting.

The algorithm first computes principal curvatures κ_1 and κ_2 for each surface point of the image, then the surface point is classified into eight fundamental surface types according to the signs of the *Gaussian curvature* $K = \kappa_1 \kappa_2$ and *mean curvature* $H = \kappa_1 + \kappa_2$ as follows:

- *peak* : if $H < 0$ and $K > 0$,

- *ridge* : if $H < 0$ and $K = 0$,

- *saddle ridge* : if $H < 0$ and $K < 0$,

- *minimal* : if $H = 0$ and $K < 0$,

- *saddle valley* : if $H > 0$ and $K < 0$,

- *valley* : if $H > 0$ and $K = 0$,

- *pit* : if $H > 0$ and $K > 0$,

- *flat* : if $H = 0$ and $K = 0$.

Then the segmentation is refined by a *fitting-and-growing* algorithm. For each connected region of a given surface type, a *seed region* is first found by iteratively shrinking the connected region until the area of the largest connected subregion is lower than a threshold. Then an iterative region growing algorithm is applied to fit the original image data on the seed region and subsequent growth regions. Basic least-squares-fitted bivariate polynomials up to the fourth order are used. A plane is always fit first to the small seed region; if the fitting error is too high, then the next higher-order surface is fit until the fourth order. The termination criteria of the iteration are expressed as a set of rules:

1. The maximum error exceeds a pre-specified threshold.

2. Enough pixels have been included in the grown region.

3. Further fitting-and-growing does not include enough pixels.

4. At least two iterations are required for a given surface fit order before the algorithm is allowed to stop due to Rule 2 or 3.

Finally, surface regions that join smoothly at their shared boundaries are merged together to create the final surface region description.

They show very good results on range and intensity images. However, we feel that such approaches fail to look for discontinuities explicitly and are attempting to find *local* discontinuities by comparing *global* smoothness, and are sensitive to adjustments of merging parameters. In addition, they may require a rather complex control structure.

Faugeras *et al* [36] presented a similar method to segment range data into planar and quadratic patches. They start by segmenting the surface points of the image into tiny triangles using a simple triangulation algorithm presented in [35]. Then they approximate each of these triangles with planar or quadratic equations using a least-square-error method, and merge adjacent triangles with similar approximated equations. They also compute lines of high curvature on the surface and forbid the merging of regions located across such curves. This method is very similar to that of Besl and Jain's.

Ponce and Brady [23,72] also suggested using curvature discontinuities to segment surfaces; however, their method stops at detecting such discontinuities and does not lead to a complete segmentation.

2.1.4   SUMMARY

From the above discussion, we find that volume descriptions have the advantage that they provide complete object-centered descriptions; unfortunately, these descriptions are in general hard to compute. On the other hand, curve/line descriptions are easier to obtain; but they contain less information than is necessary to describe 3-D objects, and they are sensitive to noise and occlusion. Therefore, most of the curve/line descriptions serve as an intermediate step which is used to derive further descriptions at higher levels such as surface descriptions. This is the reason why surface descriptions are chosen in our research. Furthermore, among those different approaches used in surface descriptions, global surface descriptions suffer from being highly sensitive to occlusion, while randomly segmented descriptions have the disadvantages of being sensitive to small changes and of usually requiring a large number of patches. Thus, a surface description based on segmentation at physical features is the best choice.

2.2   Survey of Recognition Systems

In this section, typical object recognition systems are listed. Each example is discussed according to the following issues:

- How are the *models* invoked and represented?

- What *scene features* are extracted and described?

- How is the *matching* of the descriptions of model and scene objects done?

- Major *advantages* of this system.

- Major *disadvantages* of this system.

2.2.1   3DPO

Horaud and Bolles [44] and Bolles *et al* [18] presented the 3DPO system for recognizing and locating 3-D parts in range data.

Models:

The model consists of two parts: an augmented CAD model and a feature classification network. The CAD model describes edges, surfaces, vertices, and their relations. The feature-classification network classifies observable features by type and size. The model objects are represented by a tree-like network such that each feature contains a pointer to each instance in the CAD models.

Scene features:

Range images are used in this system. Discontinuities are detected and classified into cylindrical and linear curves.

Matching:

A *local-feature-focus* method is used. At first, the system searches for features that match a feature for some model (for example, a cylindrical curve with a given radius). Then objects are hypothesized by determining whether a pair of observed segments are consistent with a given model feature.

Advantages:

The main advantage is that the representation for models is object-centered. The system also shows good results on bin-picking tasks of industrial parts.

Disadvantages:

Since the models are represented in 3-D, it is very difficult to compute them automatically, therefore a CAD model is required that usually needs help from a user, and it also needs a very complex network. Furthermore, this system relies heavily on detecting circular arcs and straight dihedral edges, so the shape of the objects it can recognize is restricted.

2.2.2   NEVATIA AND BINFORD

Nevatia and Binford [64] presented a technique which uses generalized cylinders to describe and recognize curved objects.

Models:

Each model object is represented by a relational graph for each view of this object, using a set of generalized cylinders corresponding to elongated subparts of the object. The object parts are represented as *ribbons* which contain 3-D cross-sections of range discontinuity boundaries, and *joints* which indicate the adjacency of ribbons. Finally, a relational graph is generated for each model view. Each node of the graph represents a joint, and each link represents its corresponding ribbon associated with the geometric properties of this ribbon, such as the axis length, average cross-section width, elongatedness, and type (conical or cylindrical).

Scene features:

The same technique is used to describe the scene objects. Each scene object is finally represented by a relational graph.

Matching:

The matching consists of two major steps: In the first step, significant features of the description are used to index the models. This is done by comparing three properties of the *distinguished* pieces (long or wide pieces) in the object. These properties are the connectivity of the distinguished piece (connected at one end or both), its type (distinguished because it is long or because it is wide), and whether it is conical or cylindrical. In the second step, the object description is compared to each of these models (in the order of indexing) and preferred matches chosen. This is done by first matching similar, distinguished pieces. The match is then grown to include other pieces, while maintaining consistent connectivity relations. The scene graph is allowed to match a model graph, even if some of the model ribbons are not present in the scene graph. But the scene graph may not contain extra ribbons which are not matched by any ribbon in the model graph.

Advantages:

Model and scene object descriptions can be computed automatically. The description is data-driven in the sense that no a priori knowledge about the objects is required. Furthermore, partial occlusion and articulation on scene objects are also allowed.

Disadvantages:

This method, as well as others which use volume descriptions, may not be able to work with 3-D objects with complex shapes.

2.2.3 ACRONYM

Brooks [25,26] developed an image understanding system called ACRONYM which uses generalized cylinders for descriptions of model and scene objects.

Models:

The model objects are represented by hierarchical graphs of primitive volumes described by generalized cylinders (GC). The user constructs a tree for each object, where nodes contain parts of objects represented by GC, and links represent their subpart relation. The tree is hierarchical in that higher nodes in the tree correspond to more significant parts in the description. The user is also required to construct a model class hierarchy called a *restriction graph*. This graph contains sets of constraints for different classes of objects and is used later to guide the match between model and scene objects. The root node represents the empty set of constraints. A node is added as a child of another node by constructing its constraint list from the union of its parent's constraints and the additional constraints needed to define the new node's more specialized model class. An arc in the graph always points from a less restrictive model class to a more restrictive one. During the matching process, other nodes are also added to the restriction graph in order to specialize further a given model for case analysis, or to specify an instance of a match of the model to a set of image features.

Scene features:

Ribbons and *ellipses* are used to describe scene objects. A ribbon is used to describe the projection of a GC body and an ellipse is used to describe the ends (terminators) of the GC. At first, contours of objects are extracted and linked, then ribbons and ellipses are fit to the sets of contours. The descriptions are finally represented by an *observation graph* whose nodes contain ribbon and ellipse descriptions and links specify spatial relations between nodes.

Matching:

ACRONYM predicts appearances of models in terms of ribbons and ellipses that can be observed in an image based on viewpoint-insensitive symbolic constraints. A rule-base module followed by a case analysis is used to generate and restrict predictions. Matching is performed at two levels: First, predicted ribbons must match image ribbons, and second, these local matches must be globally consistent.

Advantages:

The main achievement of this system is that it provides an effective predictive and geometrical reasoning method that can be very useful in image understanding.

Disadvantages:

The main restriction of ACRONYM is that models and restriction graphs are constructed by the user, which is very expensive and restricts the possibility of automatic model building. Furthermore, since both models and scenes are represented by GCs that consist of ribbons and ellipses, the shape of model and scene objects is restricted; in addition, the viewing direction is assumed to be approximately known.

2.2.4 EXTENDED GAUSSIAN IMAGE (EGI)

Horn *et al* used multi-view EGI models to recognize 3-D objects [45,46,49].

Models:

Each model object is represented by its mapping on the Gaussian sphere. More specifically, a two-dimensional table is constructed for each possible viewpoint-EGI pair.

Scene features:

Each scene object is represented by an EGI.

Matching:

The EGI's of scene objects and model views are compared. To constrain the search space, the two EGI's are first aligned along the directions of minimum EGI mass inertia, then a match measure is specified by comparing the similarity in their mass distributions. The model that maximizes this measure is chosen as the matched model.

Advantages:

The computation of EGI is straightforward and fast; furthermore, the same description is used to represent model and scene objects so that no *translation* is required as is necessary for those systems using different descriptions for models and scenes.

Disadvantages:

EGI is sensitive to occlusion and is unique only for convex objects. Furthermore, when multiple objects are present in a single scene, it may be necessary to segment the EGI into regions corresponding to separate objects, and it is not clear how to achieve this, except for simple-shaped objects.

2.2.5 OSHIMA AND SHIRAI

Oshima and Shirai [66,67] developed a model-based recognition system for objects with planar and curved surfaces.

Models:

Each model is represented by a *relational-feature graph* whose nodes represent planar or smoothly curved surfaces, and links represent relations between adjacent surfaces.

Scene features:

Range images of 3-D objects are used. Connected points with similar range values are grouped into small surface elements, these elements are then merged into maximal planar and curved regions. For each surface, a set of global features is computed, including surface type, number of adjacent regions, area, perimeter, compactness, occlusion, minimum and maximum extent, and mean and standard deviation of radius.

Matching:

Matching is achieved by a combination of data-driven and model-driven searching processes. At first, *kernel nodes* which consist of large, planar surfaces with no occlusion are extracted. Next, an exhaustive search of all model graphs is performed and those containing regions which match the kernel nodes are selected as candidates. Finally, a *depth-first search* is applied to build the correspondences for remaining surfaces.

Advantages:

The model descriptions can be computed automatically, and the same description is used to represent model and scene objects.

Disadvantages:

Only one view is used for each model object, if objects may be viewed from multiple directions, then a separate relational graph must be constructed for each view, and these models must be treated independently by the matching process. Furthermore, no occlusion is allowed for curved surfaces.

2.2.6 GRIMSON AND LOZANO-PÉREZ

Grimson and Lozano-Pérez [39,40] discussed how local measurements of 3-D positions and surface normals can be used to identify and locate objects from among a set of unknown objects.

Models:

Models consist of polyhedral objects represented by their planar faces. The information about these faces (such as their equations) and the relations between faces (such as distance) are also computed.

Scene features:

Sparse range or tactile data of 3-D objects are used as scene features. The sensor is assumed to be capable of providing 3-D information about the position and local surface orientation of a small set of points on the objects. Each sensor point is processed to obtain *surface points* and *surface normals*.

Matching:

The matching process contains two steps: In the first step, a set of feasible interpretations of the sensory data is constructed. Interpretations consist of pairings of each sensed point with some object surface of one of the models. Interpretations inconsistent with local constraints are discarded. In the second step, the feasible interpretations are verified by a transformation test. An interpretation is accepted if it can be used to solve for a transformation that would place each sensed point on an object surface.

Advantages:

The advantages include the fact that sparse range or tactile data can be recognized, the transformation of the sensed objects can be computed, and the representation for model and scene objects are compact and can be obtained easily.

Disadvantages:

Only polyhedral objects or objects with sufficient number of planar surfaces can be used in this system.

2.2.7 FAUGERAS AND HEBERT

Faugeras and Hebert [37] developed a system to recognize and locate rigid objects in 3-D space.

Models:

Model objects are represented in terms of linear features such as points, lines, and planes.

Scene features:

Range images are used. The same features such as significant points, lines, and planes are used to describe scene objects. Edges such as surface discontinuities are extracted using nonmaxima suppression on maxima of surface normals. Planar surfaces are then extracted by using a region-growing method that is similar to that used by Besl and Jain [10].

Matching:

The system uses *rigidity constraints* to guide the matching process. At first, possible pairings between model and scene features are established, and the transformation is estimated using quaternions. Then, further matches are predicted and verified by the rigidity constraints.

Advantages:

This system uses transformation or rigidity constraints which is independent of viewing directions.

Disadvantages:

Only linear features are used. Furthermore, the segmentation of objects may result in a large number of surface patches, and since the segmentation is not guided, it is sensitive to small changes on the surfaces.

2.2.8 BHANU

Bhanu [13] presented a 3-D scene analysis system for the shape matching of real world 3-D objects.

Models:

Object models are constructed using multiple-view range images. At first, range images of each model object from different views are acquired. The relative orientation between each pair of views is assumed to be known. Then the surface points of the object in each view are isolated from the background by removing pixels with large depth values (far away from viewer). Second, a large number of object surface points are obtained by transforming points from each individual views into a common object-centered coordinate system. Finally, the object is represented as a set of planar faces approximated by polygons. This is accomplished by a two-step algorithm. In the first step, a three-point seed algorithm is used to group surface points into face regions, and in the second step, the face regions are approximated by 3-D planar convex polygons.

Features:

Range images of unknown objects are acquired using a range finder. The object points are segmented from the background and grouped into 3-D planar convex polygons using the technique described above. The face features such as area, perimeter, length of maximum, minimum, and mean radius vectors from the face centroids are extracted for matching primitives.

Matching:

Shape matching is performed by matching the face description of an unknown view with the stored model using a relaxation-based scheme called *stochastic face labeling.* The face features obtained above are used to compute the initial face-labeling probabilities for possible matching between each model face m_i and each face in the unknown view s_i. Then the labeling probabilities are updated by checking the compatibilities in geometric transform for each pair $<m_i, s_i>$. The compatibility between m_i and s_i is obtained by finding the transformation T_i between them, and applying T_i

to other pairs $<m_j, s_j>$, computing the error in feature values after the transformation. The match is less compatible if the error is large.

Advantages:

The major advantage is that the model is represented in an object-centered coordinate rather than in that of individual views. Furthermore, the description is data-driven and can be computed automatically without help from a user.

Disadvantages:

The method relies too heavily on the consistency of the output from the face-finding algorithm. Furthermore, since only planar faces are used, the number of faces is very large, 85 in the example shown in [13].

2.2.9   IKEUCHI

Ikeuchi [50] developed a method for object recognition in bin-picking tasks.

Models:

Object models are generated under various viewer directions, apparent shapes are then classfied into groups. The models consist of surface inertia, surface relationship, surface shape, edge relationship, EGI, and surface characterstic distribution.

Scene features:

Since this system is mainly designed for tasks for bin-picking, only *one* type of object, which is the same one as in the model, appears in the scene. The same surface features used in models are extracted and classified by the help of the model.

Matching:

An *interpretation tree* is generated according to various model views. The orientation and location of the scene object are then decided by comparing their surface features and classified by the interpretation tree.

Advantages:

This system is helpful in bin-picking tasks.

Disadvantages:

Strictly speaking, this is not a recognition system, but a system which identifies a given 3-D object to be picked up.

2.2.10 SUMMARY

Other contributions in object recognition are due to Bolles and Cain [17] and Ayache [4]. More detailed surveys can be found in [9,20,28].

In summary,

- Some systems listed above are highly model-dependent and restricted to the class of models known to them [18,50]. By using models, it is possible to work with low-level scene descriptions, but at a cost in flexibility and generality.

- Systems using volume descriptions [64,26] have difficulties with 3-D objects of complex shape.

- The systems that use different representations for model and scene either require sophisticated procedures to translate the descriptions, or require restrictions on the shape or orientation of the object [18,26].

- The systems that use multi-view surface models are easier to compute than the ones using volume models [50]; however, the number of views is quite large.

Here, we have decided to perform the matching on graphs representing the visible surfaces of objects, and to use the same description for both model and scene objects.

3

Surface Segmentation and Description

As discussed previously, we have decided to use surface descriptions segmented at *physical* boundaries. In particular, we propose that the following surface points and lines are critical for a natural segmentation of the surface:

- *Jump boundaries* — where the surface undergoes a discontinuity;

- *Creases* — which corresponds to a surface orientation discontinuity.

In this chapter, we show that one way of inferring these significant surface features is by examining the *zero-crossings* and *extremal* values of surface curvature measures. We then use the detected features to segment a complex surface into simpler meaningful components called *surface patches* or *patches*. These patches can then be approximated by simple surface models. Finally, these surface patches are grouped to infer meaningful 3-D objects, and *geometric graphs* are generated to describe these objects.

3.1 Curvature Properties and Surface Discontinuities

It is well known in differential geometry that a surface can be reconstructed up to second order from the knowledge of curvature at each point, except for a constant term (by using the first and second fundamental forms, see [57] for example). The curvature of a surface at a given point varies with the direction in which it is measured. A differential geometry theorem [57], however, tells us that from the curvature in two distinguished orthogonal directions, known as the *principal directions*, it is possible to compute curvature in any direction at that point. We also show, in Appendix A, that the same result can be achieved by computing curvatures in four different directions, 45° apart. However, our main goal is not exact reconstruction of the surface but location and description of significant features. We show that *zero-crossings* and *extrema* of curvature in chosen directions are useful for this as explained below.

We find that a *jump boundary* (where surfaces are discontinuous) creates a zero-crossing of the curvature in a direction normal to that of the boundary. A *crease boundary* (where surface normals are discontinuous) causes a local extremum of the curvature at that point. Crease boundaries may also create zero-crossings away from the location of the boundary itself. We illustrate these properties by some examples here, and a more analytical treatment can be found in [72].

Figure 3.1 shows the behavior of curvature for a 1-D signal in four different configurations. We assume that the signal is smoothed prior to curvature computation by a Gaussian function of variance σ. The changes in curvature as σ changes are also shown on the figure. The magnitude of the curvature is rescaled to show the relative differences. The following observations apply to this figure:

1. Figure 3.1 (a) represents a step edge. The curvature exhibits a zero-crossing and two peaks of opposite sign moving away from each other and decreasing as σ increases.

2. Figure 3.1 (b) shows an edge formed by a flat face and a convex face. The curvature exhibits a peak and a zero-crossing. Due to the digital nature of the computation, the peak does not necessarily decrease when σ increases.

3. Figure 3.1 (c) shows a polyhedral edge formed by two flat faces. The curvature response is also an isolated peak. Its motion depends on the orientation of the two faces.

4. Figure 3.1 (d) shows a smooth edge between two concave faces. It is very similar to the previous case and the curvature response is an isolated peak.

To turn these observations into computational algorithms, we need to solve the following:

1. Compute curvature properties:
   Since we work with digital data, we can only compute approximations of curvature, either by differencing or by fitting analytical surfaces to given data.

2. Extract and localize significant features of these curvature properties: Curvature, being a local measure, is highly noise sensitive. Larger masks to compute differences may be used, but they result in a loss of accuracy of localization. A scale-space tracking approach [85] may help in solving these problems.

3. Interpret sets of curvature features in terms of physical properties of surfaces: We wish to detect occluding boundaries, surface discontinuities and smooth local extrema.

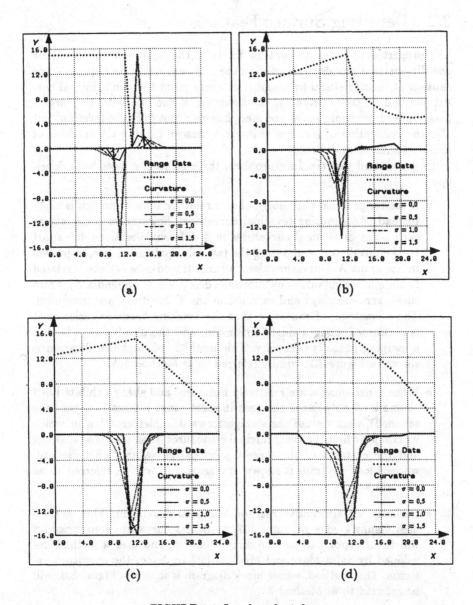

FIGURE 3.1. Local surface shape.

While these steps are rather straightforward in concept, their implementation requires resolution of many detailed issues such as how to compute curvature, which curvature properties to use, and how to combine information from different scales.

3.2   Detecting Surface Features

The properties of curvature as they relate to the input were observed for one-dimensional signals. Extension to the 2-dimensional case requires some caution: It seems natural to compute at every point the two principal curvatures and to concentrate on the behavior of the one with the largest magnitude. If multiple scales are used, however, not only the location, but also the orientation of features of interest change, making the tracking of these features more difficult.

To get around this tracking problem, three strategies have been developed:

- If the range images are noisy, then a multiple scale approach is used. Instead of computing principal curvatures, however, we compute at each point directional curvatures in 4 different directions 45° apart (It is equivalent to computing the two principal curvatures, as proved in Appendix A. Curvature along a curve traced on a surface is related to the surface curvature by a formula described in Appendix B). From these, zero-crossings and extrema in the 4 directions are computed. The advantage, of course, is that the tracking becomes easier as it is performed along a single dimension, and the disadvantage is that a merging phase is necessary. This method, whose block diagram is shown in Figure 3.2, will be referred to as Method 1.

- If the range images are relatively noise-free and shape exhibits itself at one level only (as is the case in most range images that we have scanned), then we use the straightforward implementation in which we compute first the two principal curvatures, then the zero-crossings and the extrema of the largest principal curvature. This method, whose block diagram is shown in Figure 3.3, will be referred to as Method 2.

- Recently, an alternative method has been developed. This method uses Canny's edge operator [27] to detect curvature zero-crossings which correspond to surface discontinuities, and uses a method developed by Saint-Marc and Medioni [80] to detect the curvature extrema. This method, whose block diagram is shown in Figure 3.4, will be referred to as Method 3.

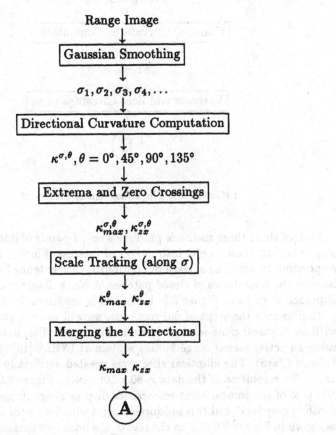

$\kappa^{\sigma,\theta}$:   curvature in θ direction, after smoothing with a
            Gaussian mask of variance σ
κ_{max}:   extrema
κ_{zx}:   zero-crossing

FIGURE 3.2. Block diagram of Method 1.

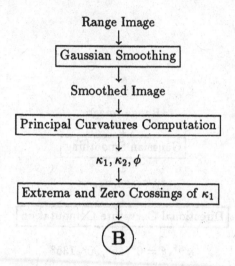

FIGURE 3.3. Block diagram of Method 2.

Each of these three methods produce a set of *points* of interest. The next step is to link these points into *curves* of interest. Finally, the curves corresponding to depth or surface discontinuities are extended as necessary to become the boundaries of closed patches. A block diagram of the complete approach is given in Figure 3.5. Each step is explained in detail below.

To illustrate the steps of our methods, we will use the example of a *cup* with an elliptical cross-section shown in Figure 3.6. This data was obtained using an active stereo range finding system at INRIA [16] (courtesy of Dr. Fabrice Clara). The elliptical effect was created artificially by scaling the data. The resolution of the data is 80 x 100 pixels. Figure 3.6 (a) shows the 3-D plot of the image. Most researchers display range images by encoding depth in grey level, but this produces images with very poor dynamic range, as shown in Figure 3.6 (b). In the rest of the book, we present range images by borrowing a technique from computer graphics: we assume that the object is Lambertian, compute the normal to the surface in a small (3x3) neighborhood, and generate a *reflectance* image (or *shaded* image) in which the intensity is inversely proportional to the angle between the light source and the surface normal. Figure 3.6 (c) shows the shaded image.

3.2.1 METHOD 1: USING DIRECTIONAL CURVATURES AND SCALE-SPACE TRACKING

The basic approach is to first smooth the range image with a number of Gaussian masks of different variance and to compute the *directional* curva-

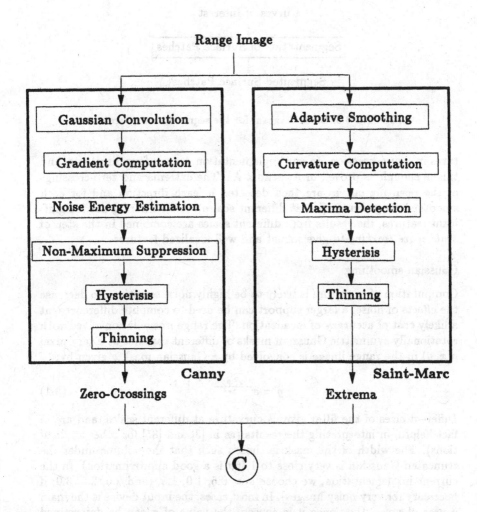

Range Image

FIGURE 3.4. Block diagram of Method 3.

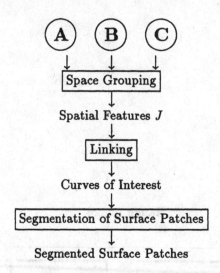

FIGURE 3.5. Block diagram for the segmentation process.

tures in every direction (In our implementation, we use four directions, and this is enough as proved in Appendix A). The extrema and zero-crossings of the resulting curves are then detected in each direction and for each smoothed range image (i.e. at different scales). After filtering out insignificant features, the results from different scales are combined in the step of *scale-space tracking* to give robust and well-localized features.

Gaussian smoothing

Computation of curvature is likely to be highly noise sensitive. To decrease the effects of noise, a larger support can be used to compute differences, at a likely cost of accuracy of localization. The range image is convolved with rotationally symmetric Gaussian masks of different variance σ. Every pixel $p(x, y)$ in the range image is convolved by a Gaussian mask g given by:

$$g = e^{-\frac{x^2+y^2}{2\sigma^2}} \tag{3.1}$$

Different sizes of the filter give us curvature at different scales, and are in fact helpful in interpreting the results (as in [3] and [85] for other applications). The width of the mask is chosen such that the volume under the truncated Gaussian is very close to 1 (6σ is a good approximation). In the current implementation, we choose $\sigma = 0.5, 1.0, 1.5$, (and 2.0, 2.5, 3.0, if necessary for very noisy images). In most cases, the input device is the main source of noise, thus once it is chosen, the value of σ can be determined accordingly.

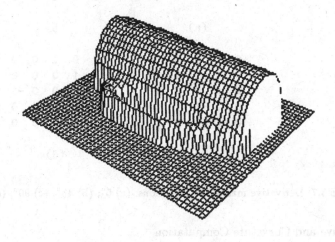

(a) 3-D plot

(b) Range repr. by intensity   (c) Range repr. by shading

FIGURE 3.6. 3-D plot of the "cup" image and its shading representation.

```
0  0  0  0  0           0  0  1  0  0
0 -1  0  1  0           0  0  0  1  0
0 -1  0  1  0          -1  0  0  0  1
0 -1  0  1  0           0 -1  0  0  0
0  0  0  0  0           0  0 -1  0  0

      (a)                     (b)


0  0  0  0  0           0  0  1  0  0
0  1  1  1  0           0  1  0  0  0
0  0  0  0  0           1  0  0  0 -1
0 -1 -1 -1  0           0  0  0 -1  0
0  0  0  0  0           0  0 -1  0  0

      (c)                     (d)
```

FIGURE 3.7. Derivative masks of 4 directions: (a) 0°, (b) 45°, (c) 90°, (d) 135°.

Derivative and Curvature Computation

Since we work with discrete data, we compute *differences* rather than derivatives. The first order differences in four directions (0°, 45°, 90°, 135°) are computed by convolving the (smoothed) image with directional masks as shown in Figure 3.7. The second-order difference in each direction is computed by convolving the mask and the first order difference at that direction. The output of these masks is normalized by the sum of the absolute value of weights in the mask.

Once these derivatives are estimated, the *surface curvature* κ_ϕ^N in each direction ϕ is computed by:

$$\kappa_\phi^N = -\frac{f_\phi''}{(1+f_\phi'^2)^{3/2}}\sqrt{\frac{1+(p\cos\phi - q\sin\phi)^2}{1+p^2+q^2}} \tag{3.2}$$

where f_ϕ' and f_ϕ'' denote the first and second derivatives in the direction ϕ, and p and q denote the first derivatives in the horizontal and vertical directions, respectively. The derivation of this formula is given in Appendix B.

Extrema and Zero-crossings

For each of the four one-dimensional curvatures, we compute the zero-crossings and local extrema. A local extremum is defined as a point whose absolute value is strictly larger than the absolute value of one of its neighbors and larger or equal to the other one. Extrema whose absolute values are below a very small threshold are discarded. In our implementation, this threshold is always fixed to be 10 percent of the largest absolute extremal value. A zero-crossing is given by a zero surrounded by non-zero numbers of opposite sign on the two sides or by a sequence of two numbers of opposite sign; in the latter case, its location is marked on the smaller of the two numbers. No thresholding of zero-crossings is performed at this stage.

Currently, everything is detected with *pixel precision*; however, features such as zero-crossings and maxima can be detected with *subpixel precision* [47], for example, a pixel containing positive curvature value followed by another pixel containing negative curvature value will create a zero-crossing *between* these two pixels.

Figure 3.8 shows the extrema and zero-crossings detected from the cup data in the Y-direction (vertical). The top row shows the positive extrema, the middle row the zero-crossings and the bottom row the negative extrema. The four columns used smoothing masks of variance 0 (original range image), 0.5, 1.0 and 1.5 from left to right, respectively.

Scale-space tracking

Use of multiple scales allows us to increase our confidence in detecting features without loss of localization: By increasing the scale, we increase the signal-to-noise ratio and therefore the confidence in the feature that we extract, at the cost of accuracy, of localization. Here, the features are detected in the range image smoothed with the widest filter, and localized using the smallest filter. Since we use only a discrete set of filters, we have to solve a correspondence problem between levels. As the scale increases, we know that new features may not appear, but that features from a lower level may merge. Shifts of the features for different scales can also be predicted [72].

In our implementation, extrema and zero-crossings are tracked independently. The strategy is *coarse-to-fine*: only features present at the coarsest level are chosen. (For some applications, it may prove useful to have a hierarchical description, consisting of features tracked at all levels, then at all levels except the coarsest, and so on.) The search is one-dimensional, and the amount of displacement of a given feature depends on the value of σ (2 pixels at most for a 0.5 variation in σ). The direction of displacement must remain the same for different scales for an extremum, but is allowed to change by one pixel for a zero-crossing (as its localization is ambiguous by one pixel).

When tracking an extremum, if there is a *fork*, that is a choice between two extrema at the next finer scale, the extremum with the higher curvature value is chosen. If there is a fork for a zero-crossing, the tracking stops and the position at the lowest unambiguous level is marked.

Figure 3.9 shows the results after scale-space tracking.

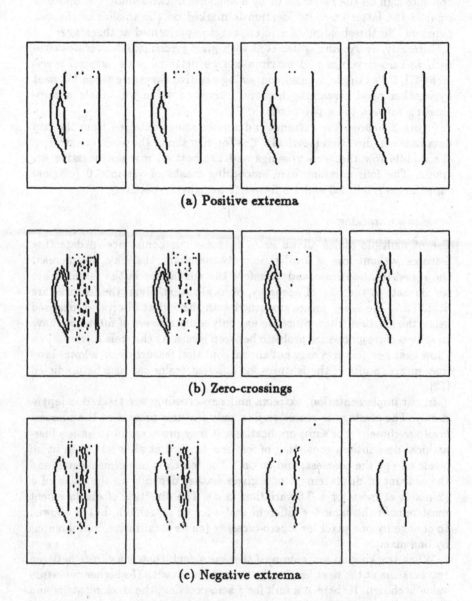

(a) Positive extrema

(b) Zero-crossings

(c) Negative extrema

FIGURE 3.8. Extrema and Zero-crossings in the vertical direction for σ increasing from 0 to 1.5.

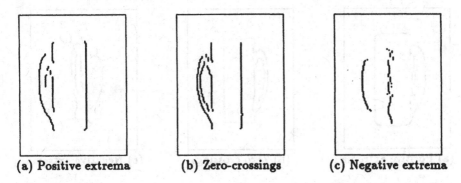

(a) Positive extrema   (b) Zero-crossings   (c) Negative extrema

FIGURE 3.9. Results of the scale-space tracking in vertical direction for the "cup" image using Method 1.

Merging

The four tracked images are merged into a single image by logical OR operations. It is possible for a pixel to have been assigned a label in more than one direction. If so, the label with the largest magnitude is chosen. Note that due to digital computations, the same feature may also appear at adjacent pixels in different directions. In this case, a *ridge-preserving thinning* process is used. A pixel p is removed if and only if:

- it is not a *single* point. A point p is single if removing p will disconnect any pair of the neighbor points of p.

- it is not an *end* point. A point p on a curve c is an end point if p has at most one 4-connected neighbor and/or one 8-connected neighbor.

- its magnitude is less than at least one of its two neighbors with the same label, if any, located in the direction normal to its own direction.

3.2.2   METHOD 2: USING PRINCIPAL CURVATURES AT A SINGLE SCALE

Instead of computing directional curvatures on different scales of smoothed range images, the second approach computes the extrema and zero-crossings of the largest *principal curvature* κ_1 on *one* smoothed range image only. The range image is smoothed by convolving it with *one* Gaussian mask of variance σ. The extremum of κ_1 is defined as the local extremum in the direction normal to the direction of κ_1. This method is faster than method 1 since curvature is computed at only one scale for each pixel while, in Method 1, four directional curvatures are computed. Furthermore, scale-

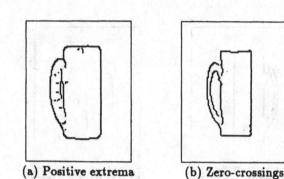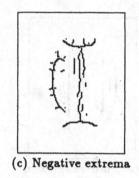

(a) Positive extrema   (b) Zero-crossings   (c) Negative extrema

FIGURE 3.10. Features detected for "cup" image using Method 2.

space tracking is not used in Method 2, and this saves time, too. However, since only one σ is used to smooth the range image, choosing the value of σ crucially influences the results, and the localization problem becomes serious if σ is too large. Basically, Method 2 is more suitable for those range images with less noise so that a smaller σ can be chosen.

Figure 3.10 shows the positive extrema, zero-crossings, and negative extrema detected in the cup image by using the approach of Method 2.

3.2.3   METHOD 3: USING ANISOTROPIC FILTERING

In recent development, we use Canny's edge operator [27] to detect surface discontinuities and Saint-Marc's operator [80] to detect curvature extrema. Both operators use adaptive thresholding [71] with hysteresis to eliminate streaking of edge contours. The thresholds are determined by a noise estimation scheme. In Canny's edge operator, only curvature zero-crossings which correspond to surface discontinuities are detected. In Saint-Marc's operator, discontinuities of the first derivatives which correspond to curvature maxima are also detected. In our implementation, we use Canny's operator to detect zero-crossings and Saint-Marc's method to detect curvature extrema.

The details about Canny's edge operator can be found in [27]. Here we present in more detail about the Saint-Marc's method. The method uses adaptive smoothing to smooth a signal (whether it be an intensity image, a range image, or a contour) which preserves discontinuities and facilitates their detection. This is achieved by repeatedly convolving the image with a very small averaging filter. In order to extract curvature extrema, instead of smoothing the original range image R, we first compute the original derivatives $P = \frac{\partial R}{\partial x}$ and $Q = \frac{\partial R}{\partial y}$. Then we repeatedly smooth the images P and Q. Finally, we compute curvature values from the smoothed images

P and Q and extract the curvature extrema using hysterisis.

The formulation of range image adaptive smoothing is described as follows: Let $R(x, y, 0)$ represent the original range image before smoothing, and let $P(x, y, 0)$ and $Q(x, y, 0)$ represent the $x-$ and $y-$derivatives of R, respectively. Let $P(x, y, n)$ and $Q(x, y, n)$ be the derivative images at the the nth iteration. From these two images we compute the coefficient image $C(x, y, n)$ at each point using the following formula:

$$C(x, y, n) = e^{-\frac{|d|}{2k^2}}, \quad \text{where}$$

$$d = \Delta = \frac{\partial P}{\partial x} + \frac{\partial Q}{\partial y} \tag{3.3}$$

The smoothed versions of $P(x, y, n)$ and $Q(x, y, n)$ are then obtained by using the coefficient image $C(x, y, n)$ as follows:

$$P(x, y, n+1) \quad = \frac{1}{S} \sum_{i=-1}^{+1} \sum_{j=-1}^{+1} P(x+i, y+j, n)C(x+i, y+j, n)$$

$$Q(x, y, n+1) \quad = \frac{1}{S} \sum_{i=-1}^{+1} \sum_{j=-1}^{+1} Q(x+i, y+j, n)C(x+i, y+j, n) \tag{3.4}$$

where

$$S \quad = \frac{1}{S} \sum_{i=-1}^{+1} \sum_{j=-1}^{+1} C(x+i, y+k, n)$$

It should be noted that Saint-Marc's method is also capable of computing curvature zero-crossings; however, since this method is newly developed and is still under testing, we decided to use the Canny's operator which has been available to us for a year.

Figure 3.11 shows the positive extrema, zero-crossings, and negative extrema detected in the cup image by using the approach of Method 3. Note that significant differences occur between the negative extrema detected by this method and those by the previous methods. In this method, the smooth ridge in the middle of the cup is missing. This is because the adaptive smoothing only preserves "sharp" edges. Furthermore, two strong lines of negative extrema are detected along the left and right borders of the cup while they are not detected by previous two methods. This also shows that the adaptive smoothing preserves sharp edges well. Since our purpose is to find sharp edges for segmentation of regions, removing smooth edges is desired, and it would be easier if we can discard these smooth edges at this stage, rather than at a later stage (spatial linking) which will be described below.

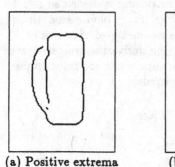 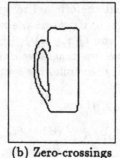 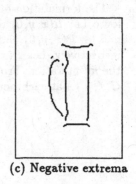

(a) Positive extrema   (b) Zero-crossings   (c) Negative extrema

FIGURE 3.11. Features detected for "cup" image using Method 3.

3.3 Space Grouping

After extracting zero-crossings and extrema, we try to establish associations between them in order to identify jump boundaries, crease boundaries, and curvature extrema.

The associations are made by examining a window (whose size is chosen to be 8σ) around each significant zero-crossing or extremum. We then *label* each such group as one of the following types:

- Type 1: isolated positive extremum (+)

- Type 2: isolated negative extremum (−)

- Type 3: associated positive extremum and zero-crossing (+ 0)

- Type 4: associated negative extremum and zero-crossing (− 0)

- Type 5: associated positive extremum and zero-crossing and negative extremum (+ 0 −)

- Type 6: isolated zero-crossing (0)

Furthermore, isolated extrema (Types 1 and 2) are classified as smooth or steep, as explained below. It should be noted that associated extrema can be shared by two zero-crossings.

3.4 Spatial Linking

The objective of this step is to aggregate point features into curves. First, each label is localized at the position of the zero-crossing if the label is one of Types 3, 4, 5, or 6. at the position of extremum if it is isolated (Types 1 or 2). Adjacent points with the same label are linked if their orientation is compatible (45° or less apart), and one-pixel gaps are filled. If there is a fork, the longest branch is chosen (found by look-ahead search to the end of branches), and separate lines for the smaller branches are generated. At the end of this step, labeled curves are obtained.

It is now possible to translate the curvature descriptions to descriptions of significant surface changes:

- *jump boundaries*: they correspond to the Type 5 (+ 0 −) labels. Since some of the Type 6 (0) labels can also create jump boundaries, reasoning is needed at a later stage.

- *creases*: they correspond to the Type 3 (+ 0) or Type 4 (− 0) labels and *steep* Type 1 (+) or Type 2 (−) labels. A steep extremum is defined as the extremum with high slopes of curvature values in both of its sides, in the direction *normal* to this extremum. The creases need to be further classified to describe the two adjoining surfaces, and the orientation of the crease with respect to the viewer.

- *curvature extrema*: they are the *smooth* single extrema (Types 1 or 2 labels, but not steep). We need to give the orientation with respect to the viewer. Curvature extrema are not used for surface segmentation.

It should be noted that these only represent hypotheses which need to be validated at further stage of reasoning.

Figure 3.12 shows the descriptors on the cup data from the result of Method 2 (Figure 3.10) where Fig. 3.12 (a) shows jump boundaries, Fig. 3.12 (b) shows creases, Fig. 3.12 (c) shows positive curvature extrema, Fig. 3.12 (d) shows negative curvature extrema, Fig. 3.12 (e) combines jump boundaries and creases.

3.5   Segmentation into Surface Patches

The features detected from the processes described above are central to our approach to segmenting a given surface. These features provide us with *partial* boundaries for patches in which the surface should be segmented but not necessarily a *complete* segmentation. We start with boundaries that correspond to jump boundaries and creases (i.e., labels 3, 4, 5, and steep 1 and 2), we close these boundaries by extending curves as follows: Curves are classified into *open* and *closed* curves. An open curve is a curve with one or both of its end points not connected to any other curve point. A closed curve is a curve which is not open. At first, each end point of every open curve is connected to the end point of another open curve if these two end points are close (5-pixel is chosen here). Then each remaining open curve is

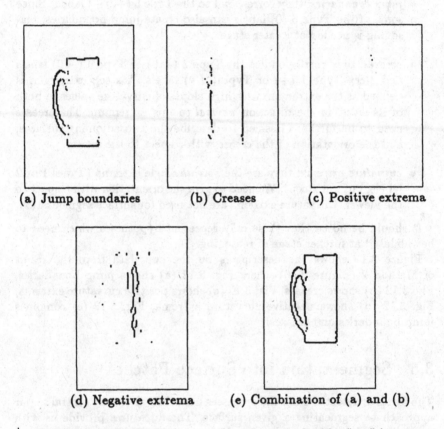

(a) Jump boundaries   (b) Creases   (c) Positive extrema

(d) Negative extrema   (e) Combination of (a) and (b)

FIGURE 3.12. Results of the space grouping procedure for "cup" image.

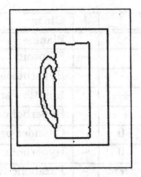

FIGURE 3.13. Closed boundaries of the "cup" image.

extended through its open end point(s) until it reaches other curve point, if this point is within a threshold distance dependent on the length of the curve. The direction of extension is decided by the direction of the curve near the end point. The curves which remain open after this process are removed. The remaining closed curves then segment the surface into *regions* which correspond to elementary surface patches. These regions may have to be further segmented, either based on the region shape or on the results of surface fitting. In the latter case, the smooth extrema that we have found may help us in defining new boundaries for further segmentation, but this step is not currently implemented. Figure 3.13 shows the extracted contours of surface patches for the "cup" image from the result of Figure 3.12.

3.6   Surface Fitting

In order to obtain the properties of surface patches, the equation of each patch is computed. The surface patches are approximated by a second degree polynomial. The reason for using second degree is as follows: Plane fitting would create large errors and is not appropriate outside of the blocks world, and third or higher order polynomials should be avoided as they might introduce oscillations which, if actually present, would have been detected by our feature extraction process. The approximating function used is:

$$F(x,y,z) = ax^2 + by^2 + cz^2 + dxy + eyz + fzx + gx + hy + iz + j = 0 \quad (3.5)$$

The coefficients are obtained by minimizing the error E in Equation 3.5, using eigenvectors of scatter matrices [30]. The details of the computation is given in Appendix C.

$$E = \sum_k F^2(x_k, y_k, z_k) \quad (3.6)$$

A	B	C	G	H	I	J	Class
0	0	0					Plane
+	+	+				−	Ellipsoid
+	+	−				−	Hyperboloid with 1 sheet
+	+	0			+−		Elliptic Paraboloid
+	−	0			+−		Hyperbolic Paraboloid
+	+	0			0	−	Cylinder or Elliptic Cylinder
+	−	0			0	−	Hyperbolic Cylinder
+	0	0	H or I nonzero			−	Parabolic Cylinder
+	+	−				0	Ellipitic Cone
Other combination							Other

+	Positive
−	Negative
0	Zero
+−	Nonzero
(blank)	Any

- $A > 0$

- Interrelationships between A, B, C and G, H, I are mutually exchangeable.

TABLE 3.1. Classification of patches.

Normalizing Equation 3.5 to remove inter-product terms can be done by diagonalizing the following matrix:

$$M = \begin{pmatrix} a & \frac{d}{2} & \frac{f}{2} \\ \frac{d}{2} & b & \frac{e}{2} \\ \frac{f}{2} & \frac{e}{2} & c \end{pmatrix} \qquad (3.7)$$

Thus we obtain the standard form of the patch:

$$F_s(x, y, z) = Ax^2 + By^2 + Cz^2 + Gx + Hy + Iz + J = 0 \qquad (3.8)$$

The surface patch can then be classified into different surface types from the coefficients of Equation 3.8, as shown in Table 3.1.

We have found that it is not necessary to use all the points in a patch to obtain a good approximation, but that a band of values close to the detected contours and the points of the patch detected as smooth extrema suffice.

The results of the approximation are illustrated in Figure 3.14 for the "cup" image, where the left column displays the original range images from different view points, and the right column shows the reconstructed range images from the corresponding view points, using the equations computed for corresponding surface patches. We can see from the results that all patches are very well approximated, and the noise in the original range image has been smoothed out.

We also show the results of segmentation on a real image in Figure 3.15 where (a) shows the shaded image, (b) shows the curves obtained by our feature detection process, and (c) shows the regions bounded by the previous curves.

It is important to note, however, that there exist simple surfaces which cannot be well represented by a quadric polynomial, such as the visible parts of a torus. Depending on the applications, different approaches may be used to resolve this type of problem: If the goal is indeed accurate approximation, then we could subdivide the patch arbitrarily and approximate each subpatch so that adjacent pieces are smoothly joined; B-splines are one good candidate.

3.7   Object Inference

At the end of the above process, we obtain a symbolic representation of a scene in terms of a *graph* whose nodes represent the patches and whose links express geometric relationships between patches. The exact details of this symbolic representation are given in section 3.8. It is possible to further group these patches into *object shells*, or visible faces of objects, by reasoning on the type of connections between adjacent patches. This higher level of description facilitates the matching process. We now describe the procedure used to obtain these *object shells*. In most cases, these shells correctly represent the visible faces bounding a physical object. In the remaining, we frequently use the word *object* to denote the corresponding visible object shell.

3.7.1   Labeling Boundaries

So far, we have classified the boundaries into two classes: jump boundaries and creases. Once each patch is approximated by an analytic function, it becomes possible to distinguish true jump boundaries from *limbs* (also called axial contour generators [74]), for which the normal to the surface becomes perpendicular to the viewing direction. This distinction is very important for volume inference, and also for matching, as limbs are *not* intrinsic properties of an object, but depend on the viewing direction.

We therefore end up with the following set of four labels:

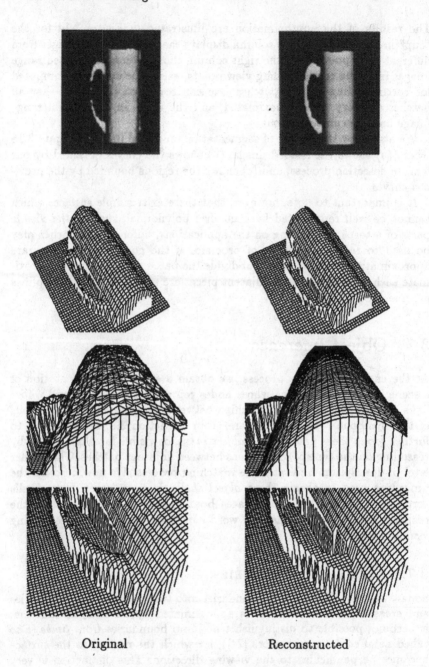

Original   Reconstructed

FIGURE 3.14. Reconstruction of the "cup" image.

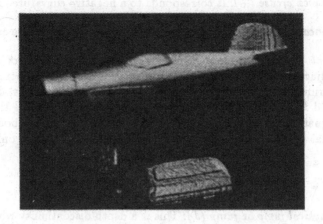

(a) Original image represented by shading

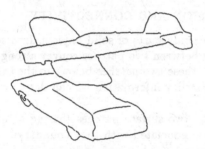

(b) Detected discontinuities

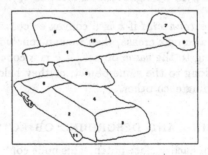

(c) Result of segmentation

FIGURE 3.15. Segmentation of a real range image.

1. *convex crease (+):* It corresponds to a negative curvature extremum.

2. *concave crease (−):* It corresponds to a positive curvature extremum.

3. *limb (L):* It is a jump boundary at which the normal of one of its adjacent surface is perpendicular to the viewing direction. It is determined by computing the first and second derivatives, $F_\theta'(x, y, z)$ and $F_\theta''(x, y, z)$ at the boundary point $p = (x, y, z)$, using the surface equation F, and θ is the direction normal to the 2-D boundary at that point. The point p is said to be a *limb* point if and only if:

   - $|F_\theta'| > \tan^{-1} 45°$, and
   - $F_\theta'' < 0$

4. *physical jump* or *jump (J):* This is a depth discontinuity which is not a limb.

3.7.2   OCCLUSION AND CONNECTIVITY

Surface patches are only parts of solid objects. In a segmented scene, the types of adjacency between two patches convey strong information regarding whether or not these two patches belong to the same object. Based on our labels, the adjacency information we can derive is that of *occlusion* or *connectivity*.

Let S_i and S_j be two surface patches sharing a common boundary b_k, where k is the label associated with that boundary:

1. S_i *occludes* S_j if k is either a jump or a limb, and S_i is closer to the viewer than S_j (in a neighborhood arround b_k).

2. S_i and S_j are *connected* if k is a convex or concave crease. Furthermore, if k is a convex crease, then we can conclude that both surface patches belong to the same object. If k is a concave crease, then either they belong to the same object, or they belong to two different objects touching each other.

3.7.3   INFERRING AND DESCRIBING OBJECTS

We create a *node* for each surface patch. This node contains the *unary* information about the surface patch such as its shape, orientation, and location. Then, for each pair of nodes that share a common boundary, we create a *link* between them. This link contains the *binary* information between these two nodes such as the label of the boundaries and the *possibility* that these two nodes (which represent two surface patches) belong to the same object. Thus, at the very beginning, we have a graph for each scene. Note that one node contains one surface patch only, but one link may correspond to multiple boundaries. In the following, the terms *nodes*, *surface patches*, and *surfaces* are interchangeably used.

From the type of adjacency relationships described above, it is possible to generate hypotheses about objects. We do this by looking at each triplet (S_i, S_j, b_k) in turn. Whenever k is a convex crease, we directly conclude that S_i and S_j belong to the same object (it is possible that a convex crease corresponds to two surfaces abutted against each other). However, it is considered as accidental alignment and is ignored in our research. Such a strong conclusion, however, cannot be made about the other labels. We have chosen to compute the possibility p that two patches belong to the same object. This number p, between 0 and 1, encodes our heuristic belief that two patches belong to the same object. The following are the rules governing the way to assign and aggregate the connection possibilities p:

1. If there exists a convex crease ($+$) between two surface patches, these two surface patches must belong to the same object, and $p = 1$, otherwise,

2. If there exists a concave crease ($-$) between two surface patches, it is strongly believed that these two surface patches belong to the same object; however, it is also possible for the concave crease to be generated by two objects adjacent to each other, $p = 0.75$, otherwise,

3. If there exists a limb (L) or a jump (J) between two surface patches, there is no direct clue indicating whether or not they are from the same object. It may occur by either self occlusion of one object, or mutual occlusion between objects. In this case, p is assigned a value between 0 and 0.5 inversely proportional to the distance between the nodes (surface patches) around the limb or jump. If two surface patches are linked by more than one type of boundary, the corresponding possibility is the maximum value of the individual possibilities. Note that we choose 0.5 as the maximum value for p, as opposed to the case of a concave crease, because we believe the latter gives a stronger clue.

Finally, those links with p less than some threshold (here we choose 0.40) are removed, which means the two nodes are considered not likely to belong to the same object. Thus, we obtain a partition of the original graph into a set of subgraphs with no links between them, each subgraph representing one (partial) object. Figure 3.16 shows the results of object inference on the previous image where (a) shows the inferred objects in which different objects are represented by different textures, (b) shows the graph where circles represent the nodes whose numbers refer to the patch numbers shown in the result of segmentation, and lines represent links with a value corresponding to the connection possibility p. It should be noted

(a) Inferred objects

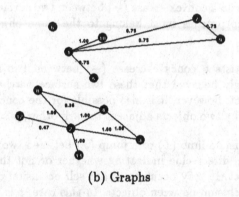

(b) Graphs

FIGURE 3.16. Objects and graphs of the real range image.

that the grouping may not be perfect, as is the case in Figure 3.16: the right wing of the plane is inferred as a separate object because of occlusion, therefore merging or splitting of subgraphs is needed later.

3.8 Representing Objects by Attributed Graphs

In our research, each object (or object shell) is represented by an *attributed* graph in which a node n_i contains the geometric information about the corresponding surface patch, and a link l_{ij} between *connected* nodes n_i and n_j represents the relationships between them. They are described in detail below.

3.8.1 NODE ATTRIBUTES

For each visible surface patch n_i, we compute the following:

- Visible area $A(i)$
  the 3-D area that is visible to the viewer, that is, the area of the reconstructed surface patch.

- Orientation $\vec{n}(i)$

  - For planar surfaces: the direction of the normal.

  - For cylindrical or conic surfaces: the direction of the axis.

  - For other surfaces: the direction of *least curvature*, which is defined as follows: Let $\kappa_\theta(p)$ denote the curvature at point p in direction θ, and let $\kappa_\theta = \sum_{p \in n_i} |\kappa_\theta(p)|$. Then the orientation is chosen as the direction θ for which κ_θ is the smallest, the direction along which the patch is the least curved.

- Average principal curvatures $K_1(i)$ and $K_2(i)$

  - For planar surfaces: $K_1(i) = K_2(i) = 0$.

  - For other surfaces: Let $\vec{n}(i)$ represent the orientation of the surface, and V_1 the projection of $\vec{n}(i)$ on the x-y-plane. Let V_2 be the vector on the x-y-plane perpendicular to V_1. Then $K_1(i)$ is the average curvature at every point of the surface patch along the direction of V_1 and $K_2(i)$ that of V_2.

  Hence $K_1(i)$ and $K_2(i)$ reflect the *flatness* of the patch.

- Estimated Ratio of Occlusion $R(i)$
  A surface patch n_i is said to be occluded by another surface patch n_j if there exists a limb or jump contour c_{ij} between n_i and n_j where the depth value of n_i in the vicinity of c_{ij} is less that of n_j (note that depth is encoded such that the higher the value, the closer the point is to the viewer). Let $L_{occ}(i)$ denote the total length of set of boundaries of n_i that are occluded by other patches, and $L_{tot}(i)$ be the total length of the boundaries of n_i, then the estimated ratio of occlusion R of n_i is equal to $L_{occ}(i)/L_{tot}(i)$.

- Centroid $\vec{C}(i)$
  The centroid of n_i is given by the average of the (3-D) coordinates of the visible surface points belonging to n_i.

3.8.2 LINK ATTRIBUTES

For each pair of nodes n_i and n_j connected by at least one boundary, the link l_{ij} expresses the following:

- The type of adjacency $t(i, j)$
  The adjacency between n_i and n_j can be any combination or none of the following:

  - n_i is occluded by n_j at a jump or a limb,
  - n_j is occluded by n_i at a jump or a limb,
  - n_i and n_j are connected by a convex crease,
  - n_i and n_j are connected by a concave crease.

- The connection possibility (or probability of connection) $p(i, j)$ as given earlier:

  - $p = 1$ if n_i and n_j are connected by a convex crease, otherwise,
  - $p = 0.75$ if n_i and n_j are connected by a concave crease, otherwise,
  - $0.0 \leq p \leq 0.5$ if n_i occludes (is occluded by) n_j.

These attributes which we associate to nodes and links are the ones which we found most appropriate for establishing correspondences.

4

Object Recognition

In this chapter, our recognition system is discussed in detail. In section 4.1, the model representation is discussed. Then in section 4.2, the general matching strategy is presented. Sections 4.3, 4.4, and 4.5 discuss in detail the three modules used in the matching process. Finally, in section 4.6, a summary of the recognition system is given.

4.1 Representation of Models

We have decided to use multi-view surface models in our recognition system. Each model consists of several views (2 to 6). These views are taken so that most of the significant surfaces of the model objects are contained in at least one of these views. The reason for not choosing other representations is summarized below:

- Volume descriptions are very hard to compute from a single view.

- Curve or pixel level descriptions are less rich than surface descriptions.

- A detailed model representation may require help from the user and cannot be automatically computed from range images.

- Using different representations for model and scene objects either requires sophisticated procedures to translate the descriptions, or requires restrictions on object shapes or classes.

4.2 Overview of the Matching Process

We want to recognize *objects* in occluded *scenes*. Each scene S_j may contain multiple (unknown) objects $S_j^1, S_j^2, \ldots, S_j^{N_j}$ with self and mutual occlusion. The scene is processed and described using the method presented in the previous chapter. Each scene object S_j^k is represented by an attributed graph.

We have access to a database of several known objects, called *models*, $M_1, M_2, \ldots, M_N$. Each model M_i consists of several *views* $M_i^1, M_i^2, \ldots, M_i^{N_i}$, and each view is represented by an attributed graph computed as before.

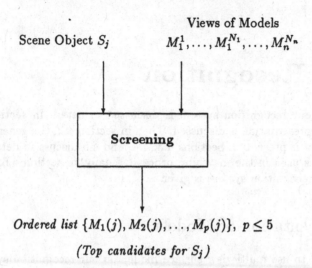

FIGURE 4.1. Block diagram for the Screener.

The goal of the matching process is to find, for each object in the scene, the most similar model view. The object is then recognized as the model which contains that view.

The matching process contains three major blocks: the *Screener*, the *Graph matcher*, and the *Analyzer*. The top-level block diagrams of these three modules are shown in Figures 4.1, 4.2, and 4.3, respectively. A detailed case study on one of our test scenes is presented in the next chapter.

- **Screener** :
  This module serves to find the likely model view candidates for each object in the scene. It implements a fast search involving the computation of coarse differences in properties of the nodes of the graphs. The output is an ordered list (with at most 5 elements) of candidates. The details are given in section 4.3.

- **Graph matcher** :
  Once this list of candidates has been computed for each scene object, we perform an extensive comparison between the graphs representing the model view and the object, until one match is found to be good enough, or there are no candidates left.

  The strongest constraint imposed by the matching process involves the geometric transform (rotation and translation) of a rigid object. Unfortunately, this constraint cannot be used until *after* the match is computed! As a result, we rely on weaker, partial constraints, and on an incremental estimate of the true transform.

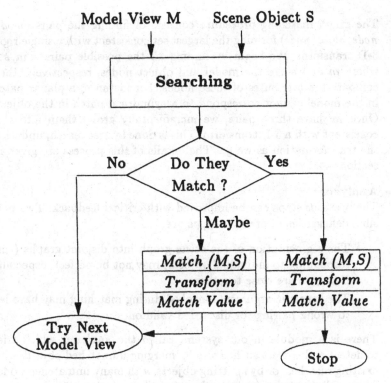

FIGURE 4.2. Block diagram for the Graph matcher.

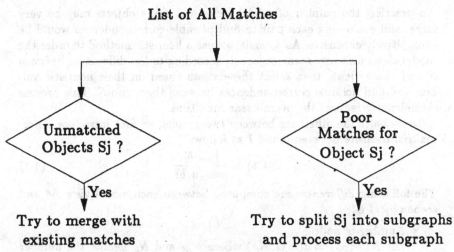

FIGURE 4.3. Block diagram for the Analyzer.

The graph matching procedure consists of finding the pairs (*model node, object node*) forming the largest set consistent with a single rigid 3-D transform. We begin by finding all the possible pairs $<m, s>$ where m and s are the model and object nodes, respectively, then compare the attributes of these nodes. For instance, a planar patch in the model cannot correspond to a cylindrical patch in the object. Once we have these pairs, we incrementally group them into sets consistent with a 3-D transform. This is done by tree search, updating the transformation as we go. The details of this process are given in section 4.4.

- **Analyzer** :
The previous steps can be improved with critical feedback. Two possible deficiencies of previous steps are:

  - The segmentation of the scene graph into disjoint graphs (corresponding to individual objects) may not be perfect, especially if objects are close together.
  - The heuristic arguments invoked during matching may have led to wrong pairings or discarded valid ones.

There is a module in our system, called the *analyzer*, which tries to detect and correct such errors by merging unmatched objects with existing matches, or by splitting objects with many unmatched nodes into smaller objects. The details are given in section 4.5

4.3   Module 1: Screener

In practice, the number of model views and scene objects may be very large, and evaluating each pair to find possible correspondences would be prohibitively expensive. As a result, we use a heuristic method to order the model views for every scene object S, according to the differences between S and these views, then select these views based on their heuristic values, and find possible correspondences between them and S. This process siginificantly reduces the overall searching time.

To measure the difference between two graphs, we first introduce a normalized measure between 0 and 1 as follows:

$$d(a, b) = \frac{|\quad b|}{\max(a, b)} \tag{4.1}$$

The following *differences* are computed between each model view $\mathcal{M}$ and scene object S:

- Number of nodes:
Let $N(\mathcal{M}, S) = d(N_{\mathcal{M}}, N_S)$ where $N_{\mathcal{M}}$ and N_S denote the number of nodes in $\mathcal{M}$ and S, respectively.

- Number of planar nodes (surface patches):
  Let $R(\mathcal{M}, \mathcal{S}) = d(R_{\mathcal{M}}, R_{\mathcal{S}})$ where $R_{\mathcal{M}}$ and $R_{\mathcal{S}}$ denote the number of planar nodes in $\mathcal{M}$ and $\mathcal{S}$, respectively.

- The visible 3-D area of the largest node:
  Let $A(\mathcal{M}, \mathcal{S}) = d(A_{\mathcal{M}}, A_{\mathcal{S}})$ where $A_{\mathcal{M}}$ and $A_{\mathcal{S}}$ denote the visible 3-D area of the largest nodes in $\mathcal{M}$ and $\mathcal{S}$, respectively.

If any of the following tests fails, $\mathcal{M}$ and $\mathcal{S}$ are considered not similar enough and the model view $\mathcal{M}$ is discarded:

- $N(\mathcal{M}, \mathcal{S}) > 40\%$

- $R(\mathcal{M}, \mathcal{S}) > 30\%$

- $A(\mathcal{M}, \mathcal{S}) > 30\%$

If they pass the above test, the *difference* between $\mathcal{M}$ and $\mathcal{S}$ is measured by

$$\alpha(\mathcal{M}, \mathcal{S}) = N(\mathcal{M}, \mathcal{S}) + R(\mathcal{M}, \mathcal{S}) + A(\mathcal{M}, \mathcal{S}) \tag{4.2}$$

A model view $\mathcal{M}_1$ is said to be more similar to scene object $\mathcal{S}$ than model view $\mathcal{M}_2$ if $\alpha(\mathcal{M}_1, \mathcal{S})$ is smaller than $\alpha(\mathcal{M}_2, \mathcal{S})$.

The output of the screening module is an ordered list $P(\mathcal{S}) = \{M_1, M_2, \ldots, M_N\}$ of model views such that $\alpha(\mathcal{M}_i, \mathcal{S}) \leq \alpha(\mathcal{M}_j, \mathcal{S})$ for all $i < j$. In addition, we impose the restriction that $N \leq 5$.

4.4 Module 2: Graph Matcher

The purpose of this module is to find, from a small list of candidate model views produced by the screening module, the most likely view, if any, to correspond to a given scene object. The problem is therefore to find the largest subgraph in the model view for which every node maps onto a node of the object graph according to the geometric operations which transform the view onto the object. Unfortunately, this transform can not be obtained unless we have the results of matching! Exhaustive search on all possible sets of pairs is an exponential process, so we perform a two-stage depth-first exploration on this tree, whose block diagram is shown in Figure 4.4:

1. **Computing all the possible pairs** :
   For each pair $<m, s>$, where m and s are model and scene nodes, respectively, we check whether or not they are compatible (according to relation ξ_0 defined later), and if they are, we assign a measure of goodness to this pair.

2. **Stage 1** :
   We try to incrementally build a set with 4 pairs. This is done by

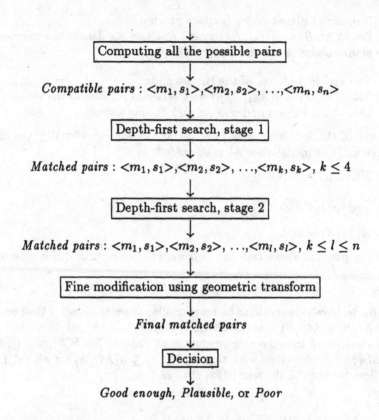

FIGURE 4.4. Block diagram for the graph matcher.

depth-first tree search: we expand, that is, we try to add a pair to, the (ordered) pairs of this tree in a depth-first manner until a "good enough" set of pairs is found. Since we cannot enforce the compatibility relation based on the true 3-D transform, we rely instead on weaker constraints (ξ_1 through ξ_6 as defined later) and on the current estimate of the true transform (ξ_7). We associate a measure of goodness with each set; if a set of size 4 has a high enough measure, the search terminates, otherwise it continues. This restriction to four pairs is imposed in order to focus the search on the most promising paths only.

3. **Stage 2** :
We now look for the largest set containing the *best* set found in the previous step. The search tree is expanded from that set only, in depth-first fashion, using the same compatibility constraints as before. It may appear that the search is too focused, and that we may

miss promising nodes at earlier stages, but one should remember that we are interested in all the pairs in the path from the root to a leaf, regardless of their order. Therefore, if an unexpanded pair at an earlier level of the tree is compatible with the expanded path, it will eventually be appended to it.

In both stage 1 and stage 2, the search terminates if one of the following conditions occurs:

(a) The current path is "good enough".

(b) There is no more possible expansion.

(c) The number of expanded nodes is large enough.

4. **Fine modification** :
We now have a good estimate of the actual transform, and can therefore enforce a strong compatibility constraint between pairs in a set of matches. As a result, we may include pairs that were rejected by the approximate constraints, or reject pairs that were included. We update the transform and the measure of goodness after such modifications.

5. **Decision** :
We have two thresholds, $\mathcal{H}_1$ and $\mathcal{H}_2$, with $\mathcal{H}_1 < \mathcal{H}_2$, on the measure of goodness $\mathcal{H}$ of the maximal set of matches:

- If $\mathcal{H} < \mathcal{H}_1$, the object is considered not to correspond to the model.

- If $\mathcal{H} \geq \mathcal{H}_2$, the match is considered good, the object matches the model, and the search stops.

- If $\mathcal{H}_1 \leq \mathcal{H} < \mathcal{H}_2$, the match is considered plausible, but the next candidate model views are also evaluated. Finally, the match with the highest $\mathcal{H}$ is selected.

We now give in detail the definition of our compatibility relationships, our similarity measures, and the fine modification procedure.

4.4.1 COMPATIBILITY BETWEEN NODES OF THE MODEL VIEW AND SCENE GRAPH

In measuring the similarity between two nodes m of the model view and s of the scene object, we first compute the normalized measure (equation 4.1) of the *difference* for each of the following properties:

1. $d_{m,s}(1) = d(A_m, A_s)$, where A_m and A_s represent the 3-D visible area of m and s, respectively.

2. $d_{m,s}(2) = d(K_m, K_s)$, where K represents the average curvature K_1.

3. $d_{m,s}(3) = d(k_m, k_s)$, where k represents the average curvature K_2.

The nodes m and s are said to be ξ_0-compatible if and only if:

- $d_{m,s}(1) < 0.30 + 0.70 \times \max(R_m, R_s)$, where R_m and R_s represent the estimated ratios of occlusion of nodes m and s, respectively.

- $d_{m,s}(2) < 0.30$

- $d_{m,s}(3) < 0.30$

If any of the above criteria does not hold, the two nodes are considered not ξ_0-compatible, otherwise, the *similarity measure* of the two nodes m and s is defined by:

$$d_{m,s} = \frac{\sum_{i=1}^{3} w_i d_{m,s}(i)}{\sum_{i=1}^{3} w_i} \qquad (4.3)$$

where w_i represents the weight for each item $D_{m,s}(i)$. In our experiments, we chose $w_2 = 2$, and $w_1 = w_3 = 1$.

At the end of the above process, all the ξ_0-compatible pairs are ordered according to their similarity measure. Then, in the graph matching module, the pairs are examined according to this order.

4.4.2 COMPATIBILITY BETWEEN TWO PAIRS OF MATCHING NODES

Every time a pair of nodes $<m_i, s_i>$ is selected, it is compared to all the already matched pairs $<m_j, s_j>$ using a compatibility constraint. If this constraint is not satisfied, the chosen pair $<m_i, s_i>$ is discarded. The constraint contains the following *consistency* checks:

1. **Uniqueness consistency (ξ_1):**
   $<m_i, s_i>$ and $<m_j, s_j>$ are said to be ξ_1-compatible if and only if $m_i \neq m_j$ and $s_i \neq s_j$.

2. **Connection consistency (ξ_2):**
   Let l_1 and l_2 represent the links between m_i and m_j and between s_i and s_j, respectively. Then the types (i.e., limb, jump, convex, or concave) of l_1 and l_2, denoted as t_1 and t_2, respectively, are said to be ξ_2-compatible if and only if one of the following satisfies:

   - t_1 is equal to t_2, or
   - one of them is a jump and the other one is a convex crease (a change of view point may transform one into the other)
   - either one or both of them is NULL (the nodes are not adjacent, this is possible especially when shadows occur)

Note that l_1 and l_2 may have multiple types, in this case, only major types (the boundary curves of this type are longer than a specified threshold) are considered.

3. **Direction consistency (ξ_3):**
   Let θ_1 and θ_2 denote the angles between the orientation of $<m_i, m_j>$ and $<s_i, s_j>$, and let $\theta = |\theta_1 - \theta_2|$, then the pairs $<m_i, s_i>$ and $<m_j, s_j>$ are said to be ξ_3-compatible if and only if θ is less than a fixed threshold θ_{tol}. Here we choose $\theta_{tol} = 25°$.

4. **Distance consistency (ξ_4):**
   Let L_1 and L_2 denote the distance between the centroid of inertia of m_i and m_j, and s_i and s_j, respectively. Let

$$L = \frac{|L_1 - L_2|}{\max(L_1, L_2)} \tag{4.4}$$

then the pairs $<m_i, s_i>$ and $<m_j, s_j>$ are said to be ξ_4-compatible if and only if L is less than a threshold. Here we choose the threshold as 0.30.

5. **3D geometry consistency (ξ_5):**
   For all the matched pairs $<m_k, s_k>$ other than $<m_i, s_i>$ and $<m_j, s_j>$, let $\vec{U_{ij}}$, $\vec{V_{ij}}$, $\vec{U_{ik}}$, and $\vec{V_{ik}}$ represent the vector connecting the centroid of m_i to that of m_j, s_i to s_j, m_i to m_k, and s_i to s_k, respectively. Let θ_1 and θ_2 denote the *directed angle* from $\vec{U_{ij}}$ to $\vec{U_{ik}}$, and from $\vec{V_{ij}}$ to $\vec{V_{ik}}$, respectively. And let

$$\theta = |\theta_1 - \theta_2| \tag{4.5}$$

Then the three pairs $<m_i, s_i>$, $<m_j, s_j>$, and $<m_k, s_k>$ are said to be ξ_5 compatible if and only if θ is less than a threshold. Here we choose the threshold to be $25°$. This consistency check is mainly used to remove a match between two objects which are geometrically similar by mirror effect, as shown in Figure 4.5.

If these four consistency conditions are fulfilled, we say that $<m_i, s_i>$ and $<m_j, s_j>$ are mutually consistent. This only happens, however, when no abrupt changes occur as a result of a difference in viewing angle. To take into account such changes, we define an additional condition:

- **Enclosure (ξ_6):** To determine whether a surface patch m is (*partially*) *enclosed* in 2-D by another surface patch s, we start from the center point $C = (x, y)$ of m, where x and y are the first two coordinates of the centroid of m, and search outwards in 8 directions, each $45°$ apart, if 6 or more out of the 8 searches encounter any point in surface s, we say m is enclosed by s. With this definition, we accept

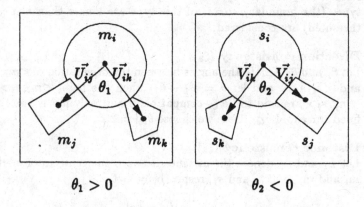

FIGURE 4.5. Geometric similarity by mirror effect.

two pairs even if they fail all of the consistency conditions above except for condition 1, as long as m_i encloses (is enclosed by) m_j *and* s_i encloses (is enclosed by) s_j.

It should be noted that the above criteria are not perfect, especially when parts of the objects are occluded, and mostly serve to prune the search tree. The true compatibility between nodes is established by the computation of the geometric transform.

4.4.3   COMPUTING THE GEOMETRIC TRANSFORM

Computing the geometric transform between matched objects not only indicates how to bring matched objects in correspondence, but also helps to verify the matching process. If the error in the transform for the current partial match is too large, the match should be abandoned.

The matching process gives the correspondences between surfaces of model view $\mathcal{M}$ and scene object $\mathcal{S}$. By extracting the orientation and location of the corresponding surfaces, we can compute the (geometric) transform which brings $\mathcal{M}$ in registration with $\mathcal{S}$. Here we introduce a non-iterative method in which the axis of the rotation is first computed using the orientation of the matched nodes, then the angle of the rotation is obtained using a two-level search. Finally, the translation is computed from the centroids of the matched nodes, using a least-square method. Since this method is non-iterative, we believe it is faster than iterative methods which are used by many researchers [41]. The details of the geometric transform computation are given below.

The rigid transform between objects can be represented in homogeneous coordinate by a 4 × 4 matrix as follows:

$$\begin{pmatrix} R_{(3\times3)} & T_{(3\times1)} \\ 0_{(1\times3)} & 1 \end{pmatrix} \tag{4.6}$$

where R represents the rotation and T the translation, respectively. A rotation can be represented by a rotation of angle θ about a unit vector k (axis of revolution) located at the origin. Let k_x, k_y, and k_z represent the three components of the axis k, then the relation between the coefficients of R and θ, k_x, k_y, k_z can be expressed as follows [68]:

$$R(k,\theta) = \begin{pmatrix} k_x k_x v + c & k_y k_x v - k_z s & k_z k_x v + k_y s \\ k_x k_y v + k_z s & k_y k_y v + c & k_z k_y v - k_x s \\ k_x k_z v - k_y s & k_y k_z v + k_x s & k_z k_z v + c \end{pmatrix} \tag{4.7}$$

where $s = \sin\theta$, $c = \cos\theta$, and $v = 1 - c$.

To find the axis k, the orientation vectors for each matched node pairs are first retrieved. Let $<m_i, s_i>$, $i = 1, \ldots, N$ be the matched node pairs between two objects M and S where $m_i \in M$, $s_i \in S$, and N is the number of matched node pairs, respectively. Let $<P_i, Q_i>$ denote the orientation vectors of the matched node pair $<m_i, s_i>$, as shown in Figure 4.6 for $i = 1, 2$, where both orientation vectors have been brought to the origin O. Assuming the rotated angle is $\theta = 2a$ as indicated in Figure 4.6, it is easy to show that the axis of revolution k for P_1 and Q_1 must lie on the plane $L1$ that bisects the angle $P_1 O Q_1$. In other words, the angle between P_1 and its projection on L_1 is equal to that between Q_1 and L_1, and this angle is equal to a (unless P_1 and Q_1 coincide at k, in this case, however, L_1 is an arbitrary plane that contains k). The same reasoning can be applied to all the other $<P_i, Q_i>$ pairs. Thus to find the axis k, we only have to find all the planes L_i, then k is at their intersections. In our implementation, we find all the intersections k_{ij} of each two pairs L_i and L_j, then for each k_{ij} we compute the sum of the angle between all other k_{ij}, the one with the least sum is our choice of axis k.

The angle θ is found as follows: Let $\Theta(a, b)$ denote the angle between vector a and b. Given a rotation θ, for each matched pair $< m_i, s_i >$, $\Theta(R(\theta)P_i, Q_i)$ is computed where $R(\theta)P_i$ represent the vector of P_i after rotating it by an angle θ. Then the best θ is found by minimizing the following equation:

$$E_\theta = \frac{1}{N} \sum_i \Theta(R(\theta)P_i, Q_i) \tag{4.8}$$

After the rotation matrix R is computed, the translation T can be obtained easily. Let $<E_i, C_i>$ denote the centroids of each matched pair $<m_i, s_i>$ and $C_i' = R(\theta)E_i$. Then the translation T is as follows:

$$\frac{1}{N} \sum_i C_i - C_i' \tag{4.9}$$

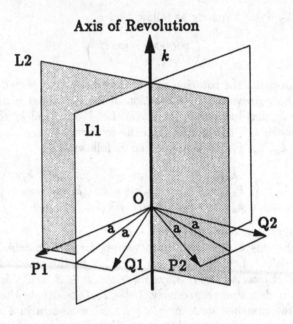

FIGURE 4.6. Computing transforms.

We have performed an analysis of the accuracy of our transform computation (the details are shown in Chapter 5), and observed that, for most scenes, we are within a few degrees, both for the axis and the angle of rotation.

4.4.4 MODIFICATIONS BASED ON THE GEOMETRIC TRANSFORM

Since the compatibility constraints presented previously are not perfect, some corresponding nodes may not have fullfilled the conditions imposed and may therefore have been rejected. Using the transform for the match allows us to rectify this situation. To achieve this, the transform between the model view and the scene object is computed first, using the current match L, then the model object is transformed and *superimposed* on the scene. Each surface s of the scene object is then checked by the following constraint ξ_7:

- If s is not yet matched and there exists an unmatched model surface m whose transformed surface m' is close enough to s, then include $<m, s>$ into the match L. Surfaces m' and s are said to be close enough if and only if the distance between the centroids of m' and s are less than twice the smaller *average width* of m and s, where the average width W of a surface m is computed as follows:

$$W = \frac{w_1 + 3w_2}{4} \tag{4.10}$$

where w_1 and w_2 indicate the distance from the 2-D center of the surface m to its farthest and closest boundaries, respectively.

- If s is a matched node and the corresponding transformed model node m' is not close enough, then $<m, s>$ is removed from the match L.

After the modification, the transform is recomputed.

4.4.5 MEASURING THE GOODNESS OF A MATCH

Throughout the graph matching procedure, a *match value* $\mathcal{H}$ is attached to the current match which is computed as follows:

$$\mathcal{H} = \frac{\max(N_m, N_s) + \max(A_m, A_s)}{2} \tag{4.11}$$

where N_m, N_s, A_m, and A_s represent the ratio between the number of matched model nodes and the number of total model nodes, the number of matched scene nodes and the number of total scene nodes, the 3-D area of matched model nodes and that of all the model nodes, and the 3-D area of matched scene nodes and that of all the scene nodes, respectively. The highest value of $\mathcal{H}$ is 1, which represents a complete match, and the lowest value of $\mathcal{H}$ is 0, which means that nothing is matched. A match is considered good enough when $\mathcal{H}$ reaches $\mathcal{H}_2 = 0.80$, and the graph matching step is immediately terminated. Otherwise, the search continues until the search tree can no longer be expanded. Finally, if the match value $\mathcal{H}$ of the resulting match is less than $\mathcal{H}_1 = 0.60$, the match is discarded.

4.5 Module 3: Analyzer

Input scenes may contain multiple objects, and, as we have mentioned before, the object inference step may not produce perfect results. For example, when two objects touch, it is possible that we would consider them as one object instead of two, i.e., the result of object inference may produce just one *object shell* (i.e., a single graph) for these two touching objects. On the other hand, due to occlusions, shadows, or a special view point, real objects may appear as separate pieces in range image. In this case, more than one *object shell* is generated for different parts of the same object. In both cases, the match between model views and such objects will not be satisfactory. To correct this, a refining process which *splits* and/or *merges* objects according to current matches and their geometric relationships is applied next; we call this module the *analyzer*.

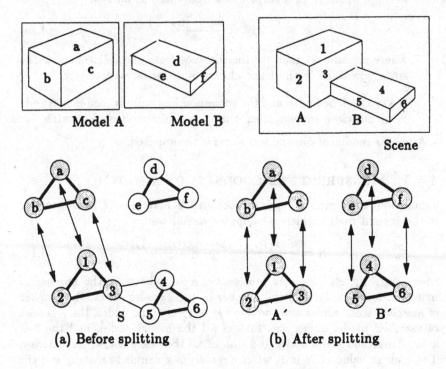

FIGURE 4.7. Splitting objects.

4.5.1 SPLITTING OBJECTS

Suppose that our scene contains two objects A and B which are inferred as one object shell (represented by graph S). Since we allow only one model view being matched for one object shell, let us assume that the model view A matches S (as the result after Step 2) where A is the view of the model object which is similar to scene object A. We also assume that there is another model view B whose model is similar to scene object B. At this time, the match between B and B has not yet been found. Figure 4.7 (a) illustrates this situation, where all surface patches are numbered for convenience. From the figure, we see that patch 3 of the scene is touching patches 4 and 5. The scene graph S and the model graphs A and B are also shown. The shaded nodes represent the currently matched nodes (the correspondences between two matched nodes are indicated by bi-directional arrows). After matching, we find that half of the nodes in S are not matched (surfaces 4, 5, and 6); however, by examining S, it is possible to *split* the two objects in the scene.

The following two rules are followed in splitting objects:

1. Splitting can only be achieved by removing links for which p is strictly less than 1.

2. The set of already matched patches should not be split into subsets.

By looking at the scene and the graph S, we know that surfaces 1-2, 2-3, 1-3, 4-5, 4-6, and 5-6 are connected by convex creases ($p = 1$) and from Rule 1 they can not be split (displayed by thick lines); however, surfaces 3-4 and 3-5 are connected by concave creases ($p = 0.75$) and may be split (displayed by thin lines). By removing the links 3-4 and 3-5 from S, we obtain two separate graphs A' (which contains surfaces 1, 2, and 3) and B' (which contains surfaces 4, 5, and 6). Furthermore, by looking at the match we notice that the *matched surfaces* (surfaces 1, 2, and 3) are contained only in A', thus the result of splitting does not break Rule 2.

After splitting, we now can match scene object B' to model view B and the result is shown in Figure 4.7 (b).

From the above reasoning, we have derived the following procedure to split objects:

1. After graph searching, if there exists a *matched* scene object S such that more than 40% of its nodes are not matched, try to split it.

2. Split S into as many as pieces by removing links with $p < 1$ without breaking the above two rules. Let S_1 represent the split object which contains all of the already matched nodes, and S_2, S_3, ..., S_N represent the remaining split objects sorted in the descending order of number of containing nodes.

3. *Reconnect* $S_2, S_3, ..., S_N$ into one object S', and try to match it with model views. If no model views can be matched, remove S_N (which contains the least number of nodes) and retry the match. The idea is that we want to match from the largest possible objects.

4. Repeat steps 1 to 3 until no more splitting is achievable.

4.5.2   MERGING OBJECTS

Suppose that our scene contains only one object S; however, due to self occlusion, it is inferred as two object shells (represented by graphs A and B, respectively). Also assume that after graph searching, A is matched to a model view M (which is supposed to match the entire object S) and B is not matched (usually because it contains too few nodes). This is illustrated in Figure 4.8 (a) where A contains two *matched* surfaces 1 and 2, B contains one *unmatched* surface 3, and model view M contains three surfaces a, b, and c. In the current match, surfaces a and b match surfaces 1 and 2, respectively, while surface c is not matched (which is supposed to match surface 3 of B).

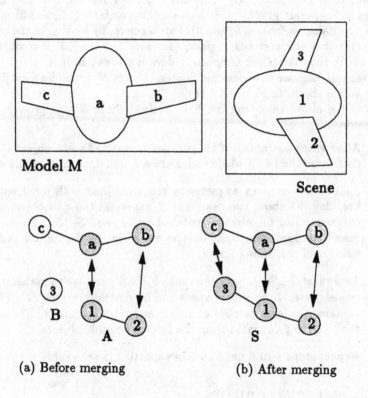

FIGURE 4.8. Merging objects.

To refine the match, merging can be used to bring separate pieces that actually belong to the same object. The idea is that by merging two objects A and B into one object S (which matches M), not only the similarity constraints between corresponding *matching* nodes ($<c, 3>$ in this example) should be satisfied, but the binary constraints and the transform constraints between each pair of matching nodes ($<a, 1>$, $<b, 2>$, and $<c, 3>$ in this example) should also be satisfied.

In the example we show here, A and B are merged into S and the new match result is shown in Figure 4.8 (b).

From the above reasoning, we have derived a general procedure to merge objects as follows:

1. After graph searching, try to merge any *unmatched* scene object B.

2. Select among matched objects the one which is geometrically closest to B. Let A, M, and L denote the selected object, its matched model view, and the match between A and M, respectively.

3. Use the graph searching process presented in the previous section to find the correspondences between the nodes in B and the *unmatched* nodes in M, assuming that the match L has already been established. That is, more matches can be added to L only if the resulting match does not violate the three constraints.

4. Repeat steps 1 to 3 until either no more unmatched scene objects exist or no more merging is achievable.

4.6 Summary

The experimental results are presented in the next chapter. In summary, our recognition system is different from those presented in Chapter 2 in the following senses:

- We use the same description format for both model and scene objects, as opposed to [18,26].

- We generate the model views automatically, as opposed to [18,26].

- We use multiple views for model objects, as opposed to [67].

- We use less views than in [50].

- Our system handles curved objects, as opposed to [37,40].

- Our system allows occlusion on both planar and curved surfaces, as opposed to [67] where occlusion is allowed only for planar surfaces.

- Our system uses information which is more object-centered, such as 3-D area instead of 2-D, as opposed to [67].

5

Experimental Results

In this chapter, we show experimental results on range images. In section 5.1, we present the selected model views. In section 5.2, a detailed case study on one of the testing scenes is presented. In section 5.3, the results on model building and recognition are shown. In section 5.4, the results using different ordering strategies are presented. In section 5.5, we remove one model from our data-base to illustrate the results when unknown objects are present. Finally, in section 5.6, we present an analysis of recognition performance under occlusion.

5.1 The Models

In this work, we have selected eight objects to build models, resulting in 28 views. Then scenes which consist of these objects are acquired and recognized using these models. The model objects are listed as follows:

1. A car: which contains a lot of similar surfaces, as shown in Figure 5.1,

2. A chair: whose bottom view looks complicated, as shown in Figure 5.2,

3. A telephone: which has many tiny buttons, making segmentation difficult, as shown in Figure 5.3,

4. A table: which contains as few as two surfaces viewed from some particular angle that would introduce ambiguities in the matching, as shown in Figure 5.4,

5. A mask: which is dominated by curved surfaces, as shown in Figure 5.5,

6. A hatchback car as shown in Figure 5.6,

7. A wagon as shown in Figure 5.7,

8. An airplane as shown in Figure 5.8.

Note that bottom views for objects 6 to 8 are not used because they are not likely to be seen from the bottom and people usually do not recognize these objects from their bottom views.

Our data comes from an active range finder described in [53]. The system consists of a laser, a video camera, a video monitor, a terminal, and a rotary table driven by an IBM PC-AT personal computer, as shown in Figure 5.9. In the calibration step, the geometric transform from the camera plane to the laser plane are computed in a coordinate system whose vertical axis coincides with the axis of rotation of the rotary table. Then, in the scanning step, objects are placed on the rotary table, and the transform computed in the calibration step is used to reconstruct the 2-D curve intersecting the laser plane and the scanned objects. A *cylindrical* range image $R(\theta, h)$ is then generated where θ is the angle of rotation around the table axis and h the height along this axis. Finally, a Cartesian image may be generated from $R(\theta, h)$ by choosing an arbitrary viewpoint and interpolating the known values.

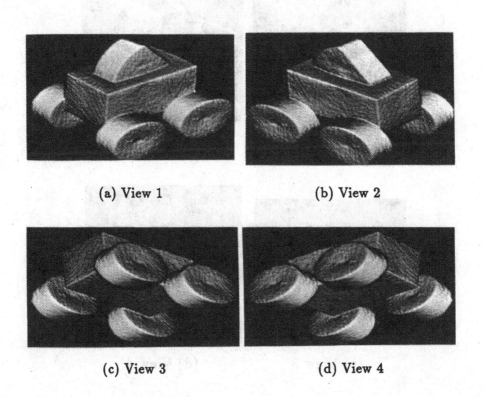

(a) View 1   (b) View 2

(c) View 3   (d) View 4

FIGURE 5.1. The four views of the model car.

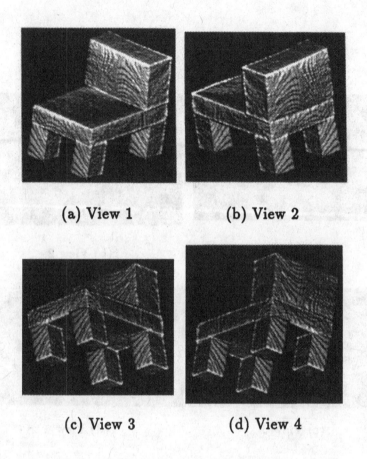

(a) View 1   (b) View 2

(c) View 3   (d) View 4

FIGURE 5.2. The four views of the model chair.

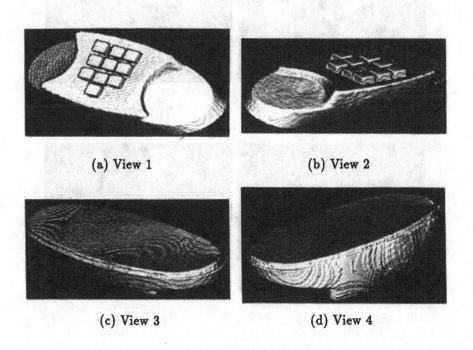

(a) View 1   (b) View 2

(c) View 3   (d) View 4

FIGURE 5.3. The four views of the model telephone.

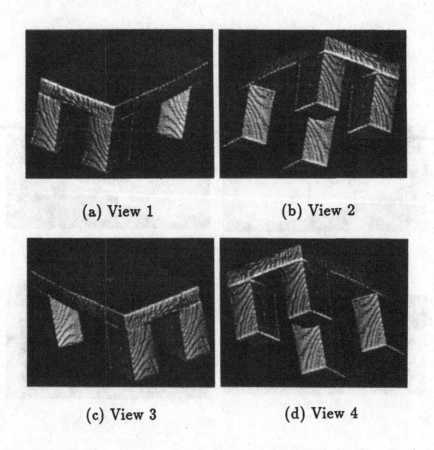

(a) View 1   (b) View 2

(c) View 3   (d) View 4

FIGURE 5.4. The four views of the model table.

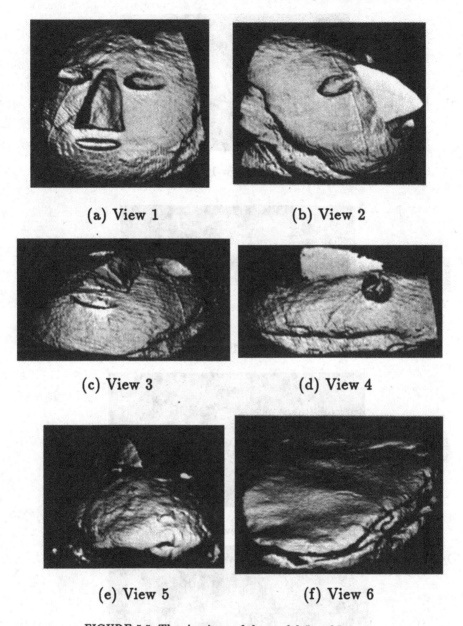

(a) View 1   (b) View 2

(c) View 3   (d) View 4

(e) View 5   (f) View 6

FIGURE 5.5. The six views of the model "mask".

(a) View 1

(b) View 2

FIGURE 5.6. The two views of model "Hatchback".

(a) View 1

(b) View 2

FIGURE 5.7. The two views of model "Wagon".

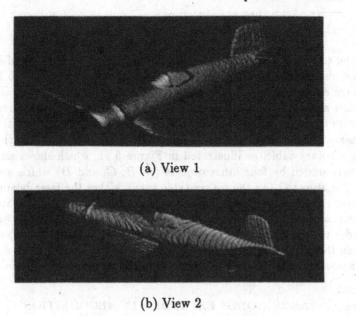

(a) View 1

(b) View 2

FIGURE 5.8. The two views of model "Plane".

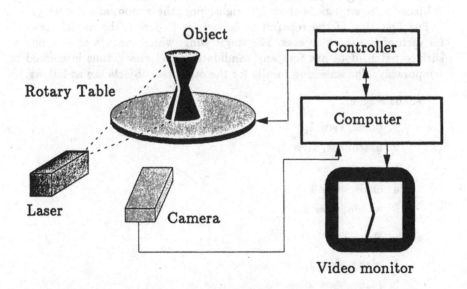

FIGURE 5.9. The range finding system using a rotary table.

5.2   A Detailed Case Study

In order to better understand how the system works, we take one of our test
scenes, shown in Figure 3.15 (a), and redisplayed here in Figure 5.10. Our
composite scenes were obtained by first scanning each object in an arbitrary
position and orientation, then combining these objects (synthetically) to
generate the scene as it would have appeared if we had scanned it. This is
necessary because of the technical difficulty in actually scanning the scene
using a rotary table, as illustrated in Figure 5.11, which shows an object
(O) surrounded by four other objects (A, B, C, and D) which are taller
than the object O. As the rotary table turns, either the laser beam or the
camera is blocked by these four objects most of the time. This creates a lot
of shadows that make the surface of object O almost completely missing.
In order to scan these objects without casting too many shadows, we have
to scan them individually.

We now follow each step of the system as it processes this scene.

5.2.1   SEARCH NODES EXPANDED IN RECOGNITION

As mentioned before, the object inference can not be expected to always
generate perfect results. In the scene, the right wing of the airplane is
segmented into a separate object as the result of object inference, shown
in Figure 5.12, where different textures represent different objects. Thus,
at the beginning of the recognition process, the scene consists of three
"objects": the airplane without the right wing, the wagon, and the wing.

The first step of the recognition process is to screen the model views
for each of the three objects. The single wing, which consists of only one
surface patch, does not find any candidate model views, thus is ignored
temporarily. The screening results for the other two objects are as follows:

- The wagon:

    1. plane, view 1,

    2. hatchback, view 2,

    3. wagon, view 1,

    4. chair, view 2,

    5. wagon, view 2.

- The plane:

    1. plane, view 1,

    2. plane, view 2,

    3. chair, view 1.

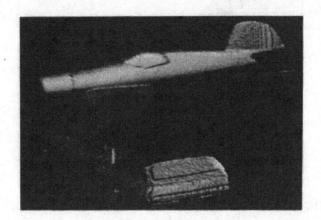

FIGURE 5.10. One of the test scenes.

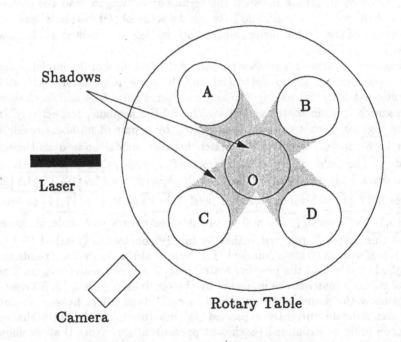

FIGURE 5.11. Shadow problems of the rotary table

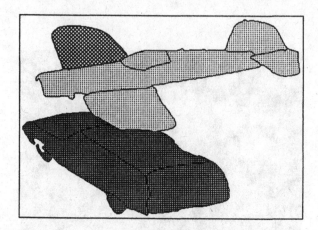

FIGURE 5.12. Result of object inference for the chosen scene.

The second step examines each of the selected candidates in the order shown above. As the result of graph matching, the first four candidates for the wagon are discarded. In this case study, we show the search trees expanded by matching between the scene object 'wagon' and the second view of the model 'wagon', and between the scene object 'airplane' and the first view of the model 'plane', where both models are selected as the final match.

Figure 5.13 shows the surface patches of the first view of the model plane, the second view of the model wagon, and the scene, respectively, with each surface patch (node) having a unique number. Figure 5.14 and 5.15 show the search trees in matching the wagon and the airplane, respectively. In these figures, each tree node, represented by a pair of numbers inside a box $\boxed{a,b}$, indicates a possible match between model node a and scene node b. The order of expansion is from left to right, then top to bottom. In Figure 5.14, for example, the order of expansion is $\boxed{1,4}$, $\boxed{3,3}$, $\boxed{4,8}$ at level 2, $\boxed{7,11}$ at level 2, $\boxed{5,11}$ at level 2, $\boxed{4,8}$ at level 3, $\boxed{7,11}$ at level 3, $\boxed{5,11}$ at level 3, $\boxed{1,2}$, and so on. A cross over a tree node indicates that this match is rejected, either by binary constraints (marked 'B') or by transform constraints (marked 'T'). Note that the unary constraints are applied to select all the possible match pairs *before* the search begins. The final selected matches are indicated by thicker links. Figure 5.16, 5.17, and 5.18 show the scene nodes expanded in each stage where heavily shaded regions indicate currently expanded patches (nodes) and lightly shaded regions indicate expanded patches at previous stages. Note that we show both scene objects (wagon and airplane) in the same figures, but in fact they are processed in sequence. From these figures we see that the major (larger) surfaces are always selected in the first stage while smaller surfaces are matched in later stages.

After the graph search, the correspondences of the wagon are correctly established while the right wing of the airplane has not been recognized. In the next step, merging is applied to the scenes. Since the wing (scene node 6) is closer to the airplane than to the wagon, and there is only one unmatched node in the matched airplane model (model node 3), the match $\boxed{3,6}$ is thus selected as a possible match. The transform and binary constraints are then checked, and in this case, both of them are satisfied, thus the wing is merged to the airplane and the match $\boxed{3,6}$ is included. It should be noted that to verify the transform constraint, we simply transform the model views of the airplane and *superimpose* it on the scene, which is shown in Figure 5.19, and then find that the two nodes $\boxed{3,6}$ are close enough. Figure 5.20 shows the expanded node in the merging step.

Figure 5.21 shows the recognition results where Figure 5.21 (a) shows the matched model views and Figure 5.21 (b) shows the matched scene objects. In this figure, corresponding textures are used to represent corresponding objects, and corresponding numbers are used for matched nodes. Table 5.1 summarizes the recognition results. The entries are to be interpreted as follows:

- *Object*: The object in the scene.

- *Model*: The model view selected by the screener. The views are sorted by order of selection.

- *Nodes Expanded*: The number of *search nodes* expanded in the search tree. It is limited to 100.

- *Max. Depth*: The maximum depth of the search tree.

- *Max. Width*: The maximum width of the search tree, it is limited to 5.

- *Decision*: The final decision of the recognition:
    1. *Matched*: The object and the model view are considered matched (good enough in Module 2 (Graph matcher), i.e., match value $\mathcal{H} \geq 0.8$) If this happens, the remaining selected model views are ignored.
    2. *Ignored*: The view is ignored because a good-enough match has already been found.
    3. *Rejected*: The match is too poor to be accepted ($\mathcal{H} < 0.6$).
    4. *Plausible*: The match between the object and the view is acceptable; however, it is not good enough to ignore remaining candidate views ($0.6 \leq \mathcal{H} < 0.8$). In this case, the match and its

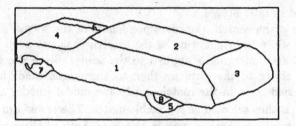

"Wagon" view 2

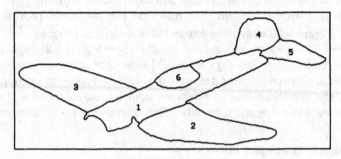

"Plane" view 1

(a) Matched model views

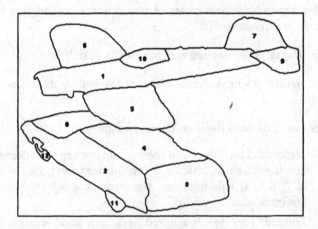

(b) Matched objects

FIGURE 5.13. Node numbers of the models and the chosen scene.

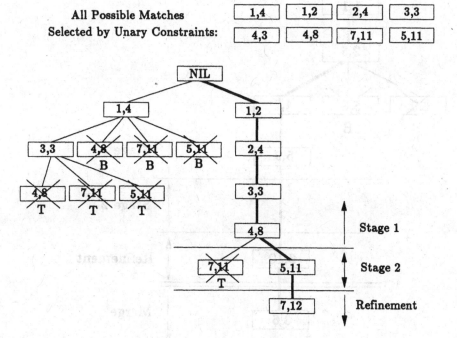

All Possible Matches
Selected by Unary Constraints:

1,4	1,2	2,4	3,3
4,3	4,8	7,11	5,11

FIGURE 5.14. Search tree for the wagon.

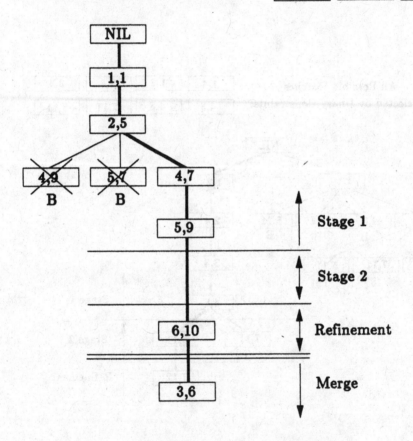

FIGURE 5.15. Search tree for the airplane.

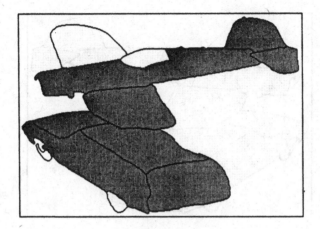

FIGURE 5.16. Nodes expanded in stage 1.

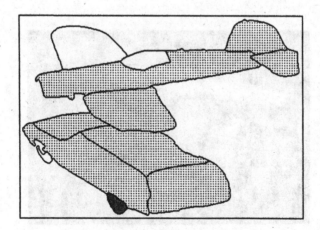

FIGURE 5.17. Nodes expanded in stage 2.

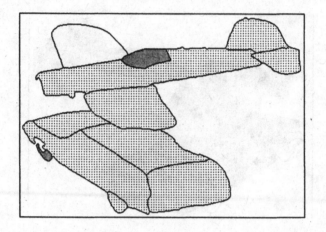

FIGURE 5.18. Nodes expanded in stage 3.

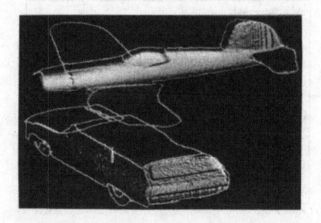

FIGURE 5.19. Transform results of the chosen scene.

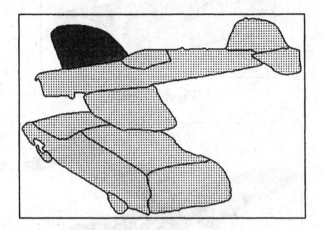

FIGURE 5.20. Nodes expanded after merging.

match value $\mathcal{H}$ are kept for further comparison. If a good-enough match is found during the subsequent exploration, this plausible match is discarded, otherwise, the plausible match with the largest $\mathcal{H}$ is selected as the final match.

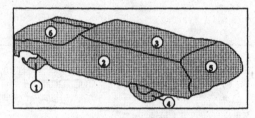

"Wagon" view 2

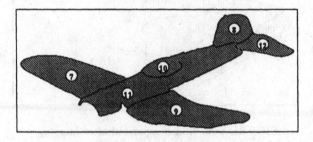

"Plane" view 1

(a) Matched model views

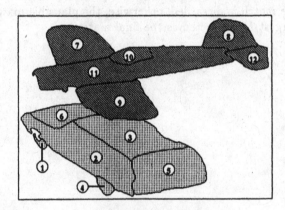

(b) Matched objects

FIGURE 5.21. Result of recognition on the chosen scene.

Object	Model	Exp. Nodes	Max. Depth	Max. Width	Decision
Wagon	plane, view 1	8	2	3	Rejected
	hatchb., view 2	3	2	2	Rejected
	wagon, view 1	4	1	2	Rejected
	chair, view 2	5	2	2	Rejected
	wagon, view 2	15	6	4	*Matched*
Plane	plane, view 1	7	5	3	*Matched*
	plane, view 2	-	-	-	Ignored
	chair, view 1	-	-	-	Ignored

TABLE 5.1. Summary of the recognition results for the chosen scene.

5.3   Results for Other Scenes

We have performed succesful experiments on 7 other scenes, which are in Figures 5.22 to 5.28. As can be seen, these scenes present quite a large amount of occlusion and missing surface patches. The recognition results are shown in Figures 5.29 to 5.35, and the summaries of the recognition results are shown in Tables 5.2 to 5.8.

Several conclusions can be drawn from the results:

- Most of the correct matches are found at the first or second selected views, this proves that our screening is powerful. The cars take relatively longer because all four model views are very similar.

- Whenever a correct view is selected, the number of expanded nodes is small. This proves that our graph matching is efficient.

- The inferred objects do correspond to the physical objects, which indicates that our object inference and splitting/merging methods are powerful.

FIGURE 5.22. First scene.

FIGURE 5.23. Second scene.

FIGURE 5.24. Third scene.

FIGURE 5.25. Fourth scene.

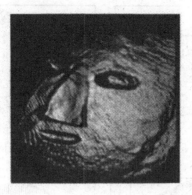

FIGURE 5.26. Fifth scene.

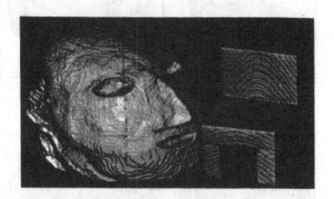

FIGURE 5.27. Sixth scene.

FIGURE 5.28. Seventh scene.

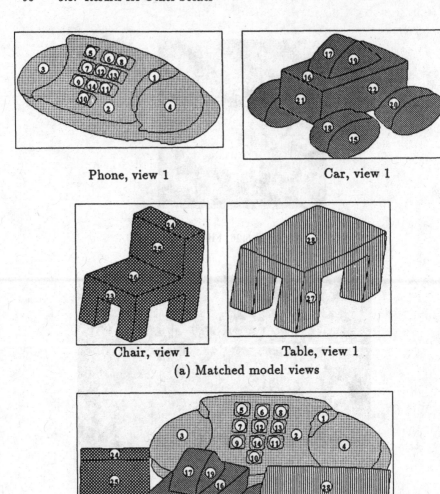

Phone, view 1   Car, view 1

Chair, view 1   Table, view 1
(a) Matched model views

(b) Matched objects

FIGURE 5.29. Result of recognition on the first scene.

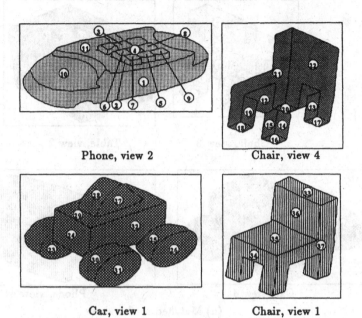

Phone, view 2   Chair, view 4

Car, view 1   Chair, view 1

(a) Matched model views

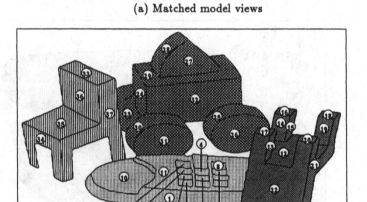

(b) Matched objects

FIGURE 5.30. Result of recognition on the second scene.

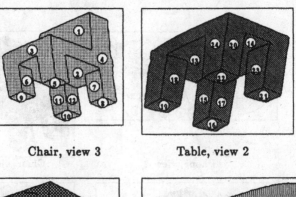

Chair, view 3   Table, view 2

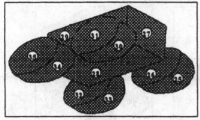
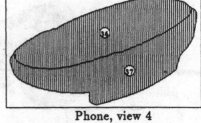

Car, view 4   Phone, view 4

(a) Matched model views

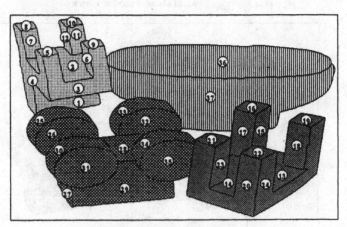

(b) Matched objects

FIGURE 5.31. Result of recognition on the third scene.

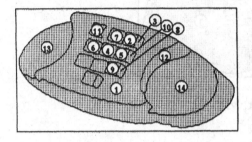 

Phone, view 1   Table, view 1

(a) Matched model views

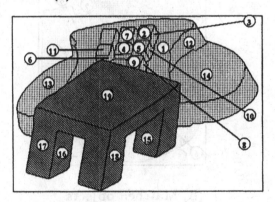

(b) Matched objects

FIGURE 5.32. Result of recognition on the fourth scene.

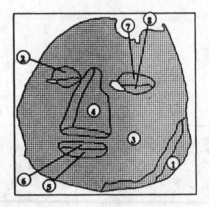

Mask, view 1

(a) Matched model views

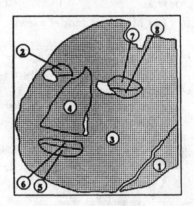

(b) Matched objects

FIGURE 5.33. Result of recognition on the fifth scene.

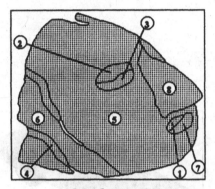

Mask, view 2   Chair, view 1
(a) Matched model views

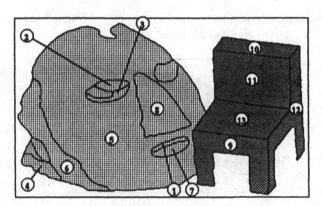

(b) Matched objects

FIGURE 5.34. Result of recognition on the sixth scene.

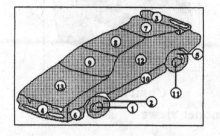 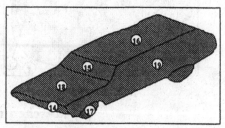

"Hatchback" view 1   "Wagon" view 1

(a) Matched model views

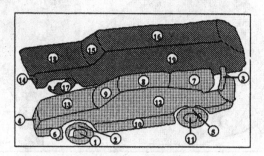

(b) Matched objects.

FIGURE 5.35. Result of recognition on the seventh scene.

Object	Model	Exp. Nodes	Max. Depth	Max. Width	Decision
The phone	phone, view 1	20	10	4	*Matched*
	phone, view 2	-	-	-	Ignored
	chair, view 3	-	-	-	Ignored
	hatchb., view 1	-	-	-	Ignored
The car	hatchb., view 2	5	2	2	Plausible
	plane, view 2	3	2	2	Rejected
	chair, view 1	17	3	3	Plausible
	car, view 1	18	4	5	*Matched*
	plane, view 1	-	-	-	Ignored
The chair	chair, view 1	7	4	3	*Matched*
The table	table, view 1	2	2	1	*Matched*
	mask, view 6	-	-	-	Ignored

TABLE 5.2. Summary of recognition results for scene 1.

Object	Model	Exp. Nodes	Max. Depth	Max. Width	Decision
The phone	phone, view 1	56	6	5	Rejected
	phone, view 2	77	6	5	*Matched*
	chair, view 3	-	-	-	Ignored
	hatchb., view 1	-	-	-	Ignored
The chair at right	chair, view 4	51	6	5	*Matched*
	chair, view 3	-	-	-	Ignored
	mask, view 5	-	-	-	Ignored
The car	car, view 2	100	3	5	Plausible
	car, view 4	100	3	5	Rejected
	car, view 3	100	4	5	Plausible
	car, view 1	29	4	5	*Matched*
The chair at left	chair, view 1	5	4	1	*Matched*
	plane, view 1	-	-	-	Ignored

TABLE 5.3. Summary of recognition results for scene 2.

Object	Model	Exp. Nodes	Max. Depth	Max. Width	Decision
The chair	chair, view 3	34	7	5	*Matched*
	chair, view 4	-	-	-	Ignored
	table, view 2	-	-	-	Ignored
The table	chair, view 4	16	3	5	Rejected
	table, view 2	38	6	5	*Matched*
	chair, view 3	-	-	-	Ignored
The car	car, view 1	100	4	5	Plausible
	chair, view 1	13	3	3	Rejected
	car, view 4	100	4	5	*Matched*
	car, view 3	-	-	-	Ignored
	hatchb., view 2	-	-	-	Ignored
The phone	phone, view 4	2	2	1	*Matched*
	mask, view 6	-	-	-	Ignored

TABLE 5.4. Summary of recognition results for scene 3.

Object	Model	Exp. Nodes	Max. Depth	Max. Width	Decision
The phone	phone, view 2	60	3	3	Rejected
	phone, view 1	96	5	4	*Matched*
	chair, view 3	-	-	-	Rejected
	hatchb., view 1	-	-	-	Rejected
The table	table, view 1	5	4	1	*Matched*
	mask, view 6	-	-	-	Ignored

TABLE 5.5. Summary of recognition results for scene 4.

Object	Model	Exp. Nodes	Max. Depth	Max. Width	Decision
The mask	mask, view 6	11	2	2	Plausible
	table, view 1	0	0	0	Rejected
	mask, view 1	9	4	2	*Matched*
	phone, view 3	-	-	-	Ignored

TABLE 5.6. Summary of recognition results for scene 5.

Object	Model	Exp. Nodes	Max. Depth	Max. Width	Decision
The mask	mask, view 1	36	3	4	Plausible
	mask, view 6	13	2	5	Rejected
	mask, view 4	12	3	5	Rejected
	mask, view 3	24	3	5	Rejected
	mask, view 2	15	3	4	*Matched*
The chair	chair, view 1	20	4	3	*Matched*
	plane, view 1	-	-	-	Ignored

TABLE 5.7. Summary of recognition results for scene 6.

5.4   Parallel Versus Sequential Search

For each scene object, model views are ordered based on their similarities
with the scene. Then each ordered candidate is matched against the scene
sequentially until one reasonable match is found. As described previously,
in order to save search space and time, only 5 model views are selected, and
if a good match is found, the search stops immediately and the remaining
candidates are ignored. However, it is possible that a better match could
be found among the ignored candidates. Thus there is a trade-off between
computational expenses and better matches. Since parallel computation
is not available in our research environment, it is important to have a
good ordering heuristics. To verify our ordering process, we have developed
an experiment which assumes that parallel computation is available, and
compared the results with those of our screening process. In our experiment,
we match each selected candidate individually, and select the one with the
largest match value $\mathcal{H}$. Table 5.9 to 5.16 show the results of our experiment
for scene 1 to scene 7, and the scene chosen for the detailed study (denoted
as scene 8). The items are interpreted as follows:

- *Sequential Result*: The original recognition result using screening.

- *Match Value $\mathcal{H}$:* The value of the match, when matched against the
  scene object.

- *Parallel Result:* The result of this experiment:

  - *Matchable ($\mathcal{H} \geq 0.80$)*: The result is good enough, it would be
    selected as *matched* in sequential result.

  - *Plausible (0.60 $\leq \mathcal{H} <$ 0.80)*: The same as that in sequential
    result.

  - *Rejected ($\mathcal{H} < 0.60$)*: The same as that in sequential result.

Object	Model	Exp. Nodes	Max. Depth	Max. Width	Decision
The hatchb	table, view 2	2	1	2	Rejected
	chair, view 3	14	3	5	Rejected
	hatchb, view 1	15	8	3	*Matched*
The wagon	wagon, view 1	7	4	2	*Matched*
	wagon, view 2	-	-	-	Ignored
	chair, view 2	-	-	-	Ignored
	hatchb, view 2	-	-	-	Ignored
	chair, view 1	-	-	-	Ignored

TABLE 5.8. Summary of recognition results for scene 7.

Object	Model	Seqential Result	Parallel Result	Match Value $\mathcal{H}$	
The Phone	*phone, view 1*	*Matched*	*Matchable*	*0.87*	*
	phone, view 2	Ignored	Matchable	0.86	
	chair, view 3	Ignored	Rejected	0.53	
	hatchback, view 1	Ignored	Plausible	0.63	
The car	hatchback, view 2	Plausible	Plausible	0.74	
	plane, view 2	Rejected	Rejected	0.0	
	chair, view 1	Plausible	Plausible	0.74	
	car, view 1	*Matched*	*Matchable*	*1.0*	*
	plane, view 1	Ignored	Rejected	0.0	
The chair	*chair, view 1*	*Matched*	*Matchable*	*1.0*	*
The table	*table, view 1*	*Matched*	*Matchable*	*1.0*	*
	mask, view 6	Ignored	Rejected	0.0	

TABLE 5.9. Results of parallel searches of scene 1.

Object	Model	Sequential Result	Parallel Result	Match Value $\mathcal{H}$	
The phone	phone, view 1	Rejected	Rejected	0.40	
	phone, view 2	*Matched*	*Matchable*	*0.81*	*
	chair, view 3	Ignored	Rejected	0.0	
	hatchback, view 1	Ignored	Plausible	0.61	
The chair at right	*chair, view 4*	*Matched*	*Matchable*	*0.95*	*
	chair, view 3	Ignored	Rejected	0.0	
	mask, view 5	Ignored	Rejected	0.0	
The car	car, view 2	Plausible	Plausible	0.75	
	car, view 4	Rejected	Rejected	0.49	
	car, view 3	Plausible	Plausible	0.71	
	car, view 1	*Matched*	*Matchable*	*0.94*	*
The chair at left	*chair, view 1*	*Matched*	*Matchable*	*1.0*	*
	plane, view 1	Ignored	Rejected	0.0	

TABLE 5.10. Results of parallel searches of scene 2.

The match with the highest $\mathcal{H}$ is marked *, and the selected match using sequential ordering is indicated in *italic*. From the tables, it is easy to see that the results from both methods are almost the same, except for the wagon of scene 7 where better views are selected in parallel process. However, in this case the results still conclude with the same model objects. As a result, it is easy to see that our screening heuristics are quite robust.

Object	Model	Sequential Result	Parallel Result	Match Value $\mathcal{H}$
The chair	*chair, view 3*	*Matched*	*Matchable*	*0.96* *
	chair, view 4	Ignored	Rejected	0.0
	table, view 2	Ignored	Rejected	0.0
The table	chair, view 4	Rejected	Rejected	0.0
	table, view 2	*Matched*	*Matchable*	*1.0* *
	chair, view 3	Ignored	Plausible	0.71
The car	car, view 1	Plausible	Plausible	0.75
	chair, view 1	Rejected	Rejected	0.0
	car, view 4	*Matched*	*Matchable*	*1.0* *
	car, view 3	Ignored	Matchable	0.84
	hatchback, view 2	Ignored	Plausible	0.71
The phone	*phone, view 4*	*Matched*	*Matchable*	*1.0* *
	mask, view 6	Ignored	Rejected	0.0

TABLE 5.11. Results of parallel searches of scene 3.

Object	Model	Sequential Result	Parallel Result	Match Value $\mathcal{H}$
The phone	phone, view 2	Rejected	Rejected	0.40
	phone, view 1	*Matched*	*Matchable*	*0.76* *
	chair, view 3	Ignored	Rejected	0.0
	hatchback, view 1	Ignored	Plausible	0.61
The table	*table, view 1*	*Matched*	*Matchable*	*1.0* *
	mask, view 6	Ignored	Rejected	0.0

TABLE 5.12. Results of parallel searches of scene 4.

Object	Model	Sequential Result	Parallel Result	Match Value $\mathcal{H}$	
The mask	mask, view 6	Plausible	Plausible	0.66	
	table, view 1	Rejected	Rejected	0.0	
	mask, view 1	*Matched*	*Matchable*	*1.0*	*
	phone, view 3	Ignored	Rejected	0.0	

TABLE 5.13. Results of parallel searches of scene 5.

Object	Model	Sequential Result	Parallel Result	Match Value $\mathcal{H}$	
The mask	mask, view 1	Plausible	Plausible	0.72	
	mask, view 6	Rejected	Rejected	0.06	
	mask, view 4	Rejected	Rejected	0.0	
	mask, view 3	Rejected	Rejected	0.0	
	mask, view 2	*Matched*	*Matchable*	*0.85*	*
The chair	*chair, view 1*	*Matched*	*Matchable*	*1.0*	*
	plane, view 1	Ignored	Rejected	0.0	

TABLE 5.14. Results of parallel searches of scene 6.

Object	Model	Sequential Result	Parallel Result	Match Value $\mathcal{H}$	
The hatchb.	table, view 2	Rejected	Rejected	0.0	
	chair, view 3	Rejected	Rejected	0.59	
	hatchb., view 1	*Matched*	*Matchable*	*0.91*	*
The wagon	*wagon, view 1*	*Matched*	*Matchable*	*0.83*	
	wagon, view 2	Ignored	Matchable	0.84	*
	chair, view 2	Ignored	Rejected	0.0	
	hatchb., view 2	Ignored	Rejected	0.58	
	chair, view 1	Ignored	Rejected	0.0	

TABLE 5.15. Results of parallel searches of scene 7.

Object	Model	Sequential Result	Parallel Result	Match Value $\mathcal{H}$	
The wagon	plane, view 1	Rejected	Rejected	0.43	
	hatchback, view 2	Rejected	Rejected	0.13	
	wagon, view 1	Rejected	Rejected	0.0	
	chair, view 2	Rejected	Rejected	0.0	
	wagon, view 2	*Matched*	*Matchable*	*1.0*	*
The plane	*plane, view 1*	*Matched*	*Matchable*	*1.0*	*
	plane, view 2	Ignored	Matchable	1.0	*
	chair, view 1	Ignored	Rejected	0.0	

TABLE 5.16. Results of parallel searches of scene 8.

5.5   Unknown Objects

In the nine scenes we have used, all of the scene objects are succesfully matched, i.e., there is no 'unknown' objects. It is interesting to see the match result if there is an unknown object in the scene. To test this, we remove the phone from our models and rerun the recognition process for the first four scenes (the remaining scenes do not contain telephones). Table 5.17 shows two results with different threshold values on $\mathcal{H}$ for matched, plausible, and rejected matches. In the first result, we use the same thresholds as before:

- *Matched:* if $\mathcal{H} \geq 0.80$,

- *Plausible:* if $0.60 \leq \mathcal{H} < 0.80$,

- *Rejected:* if $\mathcal{H} < 0.60$.

In this case, three of the phones are wrongly recognized as hatchbacks. However, all the three matches are plausible with a low $\mathcal{H}$ values. If we raise the threshold for plausible matches, for example, 0.70, as used in the second result:

- *Matched:* if $\mathcal{H} \geq 0.80$,

- *Plausible:* if $0.70 \leq \mathcal{H} < 0.80$,

- *Rejected:* if $\mathcal{H} < 0.70$.

then all the phones will not be able to match any model views and will be recognized as 'unknown' objects. It should be noted that this change will not affect our previous results as all the final matches in previous sections have $\mathcal{H}$ values higher than 0.80.

5.6   Occlusion

Our system is robust in describing and recognizing objects with occlusion; however, the amount of occlusion is still limited. Unfortunately, it is difficult to answer questions such as "How much does occlusion influence recognition?" or more specifically, "How much occlusion is allowed in one surface patch and how many surface patches can be heavily occluded or completely missing before the recognition fails?"

In order to answer these questions, directly or partially, we have developed a method to measure the recognition performance under occlusion by manually introducing occlusions on surfaces and verifying the results of recognition. Without loss of generality, we first assume that the models are well acquired, then we introduce occlusions on the assumed testing images. Several assumptions are listed as follows:

Scene	Model	Match Value $\mathcal{H}$	1st Result	2nd Result
1	chair, view 3	0.53	Rejected	Rejected
	hatchback, view 1	0.63	Plausible	Rejected
	chair, view 4	0.63	Plausible	Rejected
	table, view 2	0.0	Rejected	Rejected
2	chair, view 3	0.0	Rejected	Rejected
	hatchback, view 1	0.61	Plausible	Rejected
	chair, view 4	0.54	Rejected	Rejected
	table, view 2	0.0	Rejected	Rejected
3	mask, view 6	0.0	Rejected	Rejected
4	chair, view 3	0.0	Rejected	Rejected
	hatchback, view 1	0.61	Plausible	Rejected

TABLE 5.17. Results of recognition with unknown objects.

1. There are two types of surface patches: *significant* (or *large*) surface patches and *insignificant* (or *small*) surface patches.

2. Let N denote the ratio of the total 3-D area of the large patches to that of small patches. We assume $N > 1$.

3. The match is perfect if the correspondent patches are not completely missing. That is, the analysis is based on the *best* condition.

4. Three types of recognition results are given:

   - Matched: the match is good enough that no further search is necessary,

   - Plausible: further search is needed before a decision can be made, and

   - Rejected: the match is so poor that it should be discarded.

   The analysis is performed as follows: For each fixed ratio N, we increase the ratio of occlusion independently for both large and small patches, the information is brought into our recognition procedures, and the result of recognition is computed based on this information. Finally, a two-dimensional figure is obtained as shown in Figure 5.36 where black, grey, and white regions denote *matched*, *plausible*, and *rejected* results, respectively. The horizontal axis denotes the average occlusion ratio for large patches and the vertical axis denotes that of small patches. Figure 5.36, for example, tells us that when $N = 5$, for a "good-enough" match, the largest allowable occlusion for large and small regions are 0.37 and 0.75,

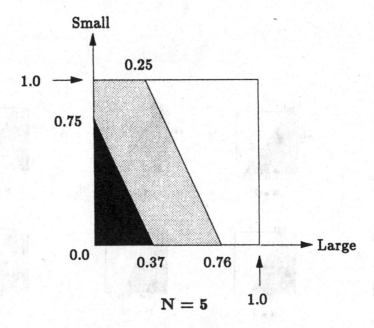

FIGURE 5.36. Statistics example on occlusion.

respectively. However, these two values are not independent; in fact, the area bounded by the triangle 0.0–0.37–0.75 is where a good-enough match can be achieved. The figure also tells us that, for example, even if all the small regions are completely occluded, the match is still achievable if the occlusion ratio for large regions is less than 0.25.

Figure 5.37 shows the result of the occlusion statistics for different N values. As we may see, the figure is symmetric when $N = 1$ and becomes stable when N is larger than 100. From the figures we can draw some conclusions:

- The occlusion can be as large as two thirds for significant patches while a plausible match is still achievable, as shown in the figure when N is large enough.

- When occlusion is less than one third for significant patches, a good enough match is always obtainable.

- At least a plausible match is obtainable even when all the insignificant patches are heavily occluded or completely missing, the worst case is when $N = 1$.

- When N is large enough, a good enough match is still possible even when all the insignificant patches are missing.

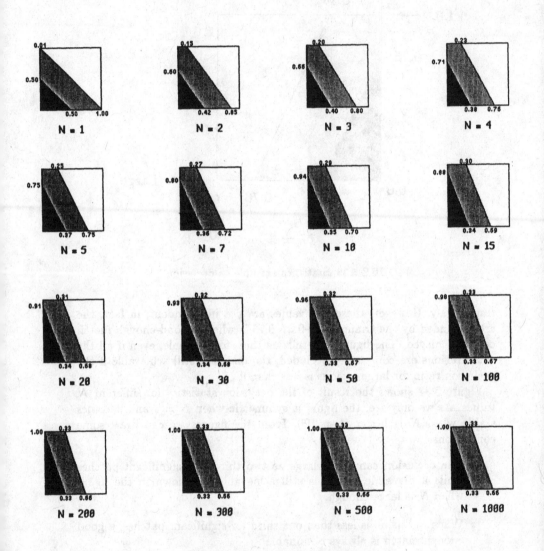

FIGURE 5.37. Statistics on occlusion.

From the above analysis, we can state that our method is quite robust with respect to occlusion.

6

Discussion and Conclusion

In this book, we have presented a complete system to describe and recognize
3-D objects. We start by segmenting 3-D faces of objects by detecting the
significant curvature features of the surfaces, then extending these features
to form curves of interest. The curves are used to segment the surfaces
into individual patches, each of them approximated by a simple quadric
equation. At the next step, graphs are used to describe objects. The nodes
of the graphs represent the information about the surface patches, and the
links represent their relationships. Partial objects are also inferred from the
information in the graphs. Finally, multi-view models are built to recognize
scenes of 3-D objects. Complicated objects with occlusion were tested and
the results are very impressive.

However, the method is not perfect and can be improved in many places.
In the first section of this final chapter, major criticisms are addressed
and possible extensions are discussed. Then, in the second section, the
key contributions of the research are summarized. Finally, possible future
research directions are addressed in the last section.

6.1 Discussion

6.1.1 PROBLEMS OF SEGMENTATION

The result of segmentation crucially relies on the detection of the significant
features. These features are connected to form curves of interest, and finally
those curves are extended to segment the surfaces into individual surface
patches. We assume that each surface patch can be well approximated by
a simple quadric equation. However, there exist certain types of surfaces
whose boundaries are not obvious. One example is shown in Figure 6.1,
where A, B, C, and D are four simple surface patches that can not be
segmented by our method, nor can their union surface S be approximated
by a simple quadric equation. Another example is shown in Figure 6.2 where
(a) shows the original image of a toy car and (b) shows the extended curves
for segmentation. Unfortunately, the hood, top and the side of the car can
not be separated because they are *smoothly* connected and no significant
features can be detected.

A region growing approach presented by Besl and Jain [10,12] may help
in solving this problem. In their method, *seed* regions are selected based
on different Gaussian curvature signs and these regions are grown to form
larger patches that can be approximated by polynomial equations up to the

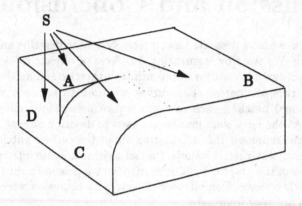

FIGURE 6.1. One of the objects that can not be well segmented.

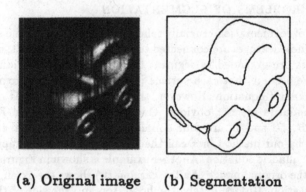

(a) Original image   (b) Segmentation

FIGURE 6.2. A toy car that can not be well segmented.

fourth degree. A possible way is to use our method to obtain major surface patches first, then, for those patches that can not be approximated well by quadric equations, apply Besl and Jain's growing method to find further possible segmentation. However, the growing process may be restricted such that the regions may not grow across pre-detected boundaries. Other solutions may include finding possible segmentation at the place where largest surface fitting error occurs, or using other features such as *smooth curvature extrema* described in Chapter 3 to help further segmentation.

6.1.2   PROBLEMS OF APPROXIMATION

In this book, we approximate each surface patch by a planar or quadric surface. However, as mentioned earlier in section 3.5, there exist simple surfaces which can not be well represented by such a polynomial, such as the visible parts of a torus. Furthermore, no physical edges exist within these patches that can be used for further segmentation. Depending on the applications, different approaches may be used to resolve this type of problem: If the goal is indeed accurate approximation, then we could subdivide the patch arbitrarily and approximate each subpatch so that adjacent pieces are smoothly joined. B-splines are good candidates. It should be noted that such arbitrary approximation methods are used only when the above situation occurs and should not be used elsewhere.

The second problem of approximation is illustrated in Figure 6.3, where S is a very narrow region which is part of a cylinder C. However, since S is very narrow, the approximation of S will become ambiguous in the sense that S can also be approximated by a plane L without introducing too much error. This problem happens in the example shown in Figure 6.4, where (a) shows a coffee cup and (b) shows the segmentation. The handle of the coffee cup can be approximated by a planar surface without introducing too much error. Unfortunately, if we try to recognize the coffee cup from a different point of view, the inaccurate planar approximation of the handle may introduce inconsistencies during the matching process.

It is almost impossible to solve such problem by the approximation method itself. In order to reduce the inconsistency during matching or recognition process, one of the possible approaches is to mark the region as *narrow* and do not use the approximation results in the matching process. The other possible solution is to find the major properties of narrow regions such as local symmetries [21], and use such properties to match descriptions, instead of approximating them by polynomial equations.

6.2   Contribution

This research has provided a complete method to describe and recognize 3-D objects, using the surface information of these objects. The key con-

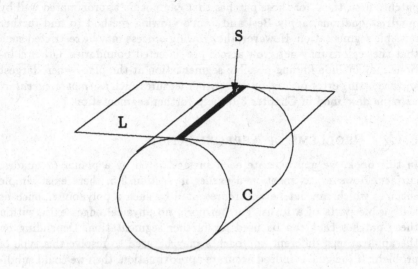

FIGURE 6.3. Approximation problem with narrow regions.

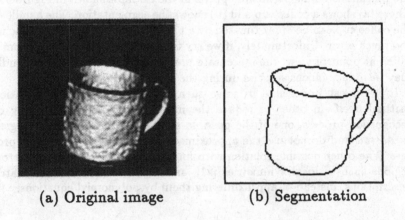

(a) Original image   (b) Segmentation

FIGURE 6.4. Example of approximation problem with narrow regions.

tributions of this research are summarized as follows:

- It provides a complete system to describe and recognize 3-D objects. We present a set of techniques to retrieve significant features of 3-D objects, describe them, match the descriptions, build the models in multi-views, and finally recognize them.

- It is data-driven in that no a priori scene knowledge is required. The descriptions of the objects are computed without any knowledge about existing models, which is important when the environment is unknown, or the number of interesting objects is large.

- Moderately complex objects can be well described and matched. A large number of different objects were tested and good results were obtained. These objects vary in size, shape, and complexity. Some of them are highly symmetric while others are different from every view point. This shows the generality and robustness of our method.

- Partially occluded objects can be well described and matched. Occlusion is one of the major problems in computer vision. The method presented here tackles this problem in a very effective way. More than two thirds of the surfaces can be heavily occluded or completely missing and a plausible match is still achievable.

6.3   Future Research

Some possible future research areas are discussed below.

6.3.1   FROM SURFACE TO VOLUME

Volume representations such as generalized cylinders [64,74] may be obtained from our surface descriptions in two ways:

- From object to volume:
  From our object inference module, we obtain a group of surfaces that possibly belong to the same object. These *object shells* can help to infer further volumetric information.

- From multi-view to volume:
  Surfaces from different view points can be used to provide true volumetric information. For example, if the transform between each pair of views is known, then a volume can be obtained by *pasting* each surface patch from different views to its correct 3-D location and orientation. This would prove very useful for automatic model-building.

6.3.2 APPLICATIONS

The method is general enough to be applied to many other fields. Several possible areas are listed below:

- Object inspection:
  The difference between object recognition and object inspection is that the latter assumes that the objects under inspection are already known and they are always placed in stable environments. However, problems such as occlusion and registration still exist. Our method can serve as an important step in object inspection. For example, the method can be used to first represent the model, either automatically or manually, and then to compare the description obtained from the object under inspection. Furthermore, if only certain parts of the object need to be inspected, the problem can be further simplified by only representing and detecting those parts of the object.

- Computer graphics:
  In the field of computer graphics, acquiring and representing a complex object is a difficult problem. Therefore, as opposed to computer vision, models in computer graphics are usually represented by simpler synthetic components. Our method can be used, at least partially automatically, to generate the description of a complex object by taking a range image of a similar real object and processing it. The description obtained can be further modified, probably with the help of a user.

Appendix A

Directional Curvatures

In this appendix, we show that, at every point, computing the principal curvatures (κ_1, κ_2) and their orientation α is equivalent to computing curvature in 4 different directions $45°$ apart $(\kappa_0, \kappa_{45}, \kappa_{90}, \kappa_{135})$. Figure A.1 gives a geometric illustration for the case where κ_1 and κ_2 are positive.

Computing curvature in any direction ϕ from the principal curvatures is easy:

$$\kappa_\phi = \kappa_1 \cos^2(\phi - \alpha) + \kappa_2 \sin^2(\phi - \alpha) \tag{A.1}$$

Going the other way is as follows:

$$\kappa_0 = \kappa_1 \cos^2 \alpha + \kappa_2 \sin^2 \alpha \tag{A.2}$$

$$\kappa_{90} = \kappa_1 \sin^2 \alpha + \kappa_2 \cos^2 \alpha \tag{A.3}$$

$$\kappa_{45} = \kappa_1 \cos^2(\frac{\pi}{4} - \alpha) + \kappa_2 \sin^2(\frac{\pi}{4} - \alpha) \tag{A.4}$$

$$\kappa_{135} = \kappa_1 \sin^2(\frac{\pi}{4} - \alpha) + \kappa_2 \cos^2(\frac{\pi}{4} - \alpha) \tag{A.5}$$

(A.4) and (A.5) can be rewritten as:

$$2\kappa_{45} = \kappa_1 + \kappa_2 + (\kappa_1 - \kappa_2) \sin(2\alpha) \tag{A.6}$$

$$2\kappa_{135} = \kappa_1 + \kappa_2 - (\kappa_1 - \kappa_2) \sin(2\alpha) \tag{A.7}$$

Adding (A.2) through (A.5), we get

$$\kappa_1 + \kappa_2 = \frac{1}{2}(\kappa_0 + \kappa_{45} + \kappa_{90} + \kappa_{135}) \tag{A.8}$$

Multiplying (A.2) by (A.3) and (A.4) by (A.5) yield:

$$\begin{aligned} \kappa_0 \kappa_{90} &= \kappa_1 \kappa_2 (\cos^4 \alpha + \sin^4 \alpha) + (\kappa_1^2 + \kappa_2^2) \cos^2 \alpha \sin^2 \alpha \\ &= \kappa_1 \kappa_2 + (\kappa_1 - \kappa_2)^2 \cos^2 \alpha \sin^2 \alpha \\ &= \kappa_1 \kappa_2 + \tfrac{1}{4}(\kappa_1 - \kappa_2)^2 \sin^2 2\alpha \end{aligned} \tag{A.9}$$

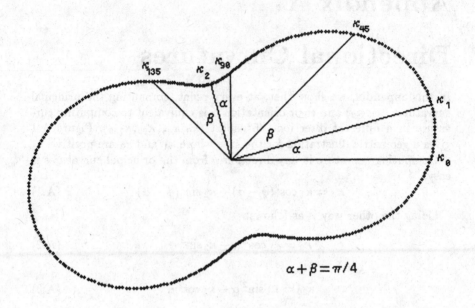

FIGURE A.1. Relation between principal curvatures and directional curvatures.

$$\kappa_{45}\kappa_{135} = \kappa_1\kappa_2\left(\cos^4(\tfrac{\pi}{4} - \alpha) + \sin^4(\tfrac{\pi}{4} - \alpha)\right)$$

$$+(\kappa_1^2 + \kappa_2^2)\cos^2(\tfrac{\pi}{4} - \alpha)\sin^2(\tfrac{\pi}{4} - \alpha)$$

$$= \kappa_1\kappa_2 + (\kappa_1 - \kappa_2)^2\cos^2(\tfrac{\pi}{4} - \alpha)\sin^2(\tfrac{\pi}{4} - \alpha) \qquad (A.10)$$

$$= \kappa_1\kappa_2 + \tfrac{1}{4}(\kappa_1 - \kappa_2)^2\sin^2(\tfrac{\pi}{2} - 2\alpha)$$

$$= \kappa_1\kappa_2 + \tfrac{1}{4}(\kappa_1 - \kappa_2)^2\cos^2 2\alpha$$

Adding (A.9) and (A.10) and multiplying by 4:

$$4(\kappa_0\kappa_{90} + \kappa_{45}\kappa_{135}) = 8\kappa_1\kappa_2 + (\kappa_1 - \kappa_2)^2$$
$$= 4\kappa_1\kappa_2 + (\kappa_1 + \kappa_2)^2 \qquad (A.11)$$

We now have $P = \kappa_1\kappa_2$ and $S = \kappa_1 + \kappa_2$, therefore κ_1 and κ_2 are solutions of the equation

$$x^2 - Sx + P = 0 \qquad (A.12)$$

and, by convention, we have $|\kappa_1| > |\kappa_2|$, all is left is to find the value of $\alpha \bmod \pi$.

Rewriting (A.2) as

$$\kappa_0 = \kappa_1 + (\kappa_2 - \kappa_1)\sin^2\alpha \tag{A.13}$$

gives us 2 solutions for α: α and $\pi - \alpha$
And (A.6)

$$2\kappa_{45} = \kappa_1 + \kappa_2 + (\kappa_1 - \kappa_2)\sin 2\alpha \tag{A.14}$$

gives us 2 solutions for α: α and $\frac{\pi}{2} - \alpha$. The intersection of these 2 sets of equations gives us a unique solution for $\alpha \bmod \pi$.

Appendix B

Surface Curvature

In this appendix, we compute the directional *surface* curvature κ_ϕ^N of a given surface point ρ along a given direction ϕ. In Figure B.1, we show the relationships between κ_ϕ^N and the curvature κ_ϕ, which is the curvature of the curve generated by the surface and the cutting plane P (in the direction ϕ) at ρ. We have

$$\kappa_\phi^N = \kappa_\phi \cos \eta \tag{B.1}$$

where η is the angle between P and the surface normal $\vec{N}$ at ρ. From [57], we have

$$\kappa_\phi = -\frac{f_\phi''}{(1 + f_\phi'^2)^{3/2}} \tag{B.2}$$

Let p and q represent the first derivatives at ρ in the horizontal and vertical directions, respectively. Thus we have

$$\vec{N} = (p, q, -1) \tag{B.3}$$

$$P : x \sin \phi - y \cos \phi + c = 0 \tag{B.4}$$

where c is a constant. And,

$$\cos \eta = \cos(\frac{\pi}{2} - \cos^{-1} \frac{p \sin \phi + q \cos \phi}{\sqrt{1 + p^2 + q^2}})$$

$$= \sqrt{\frac{1 + (p \cos \phi - q \sin \phi)^2}{1 + p^2 + q^2}} \tag{B.5}$$

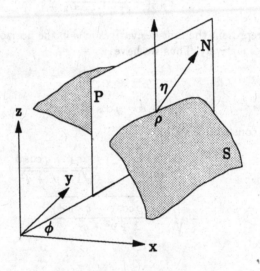

FIGURE B.1. Surface curvature.

Appendix C

Approximation by Quadric Surfaces

As discussed in Chapter 3, the approximating function for the quadric surface is:

$$F(x, y, z) = ax^2 + by^2 + cz^2 + dxy + eyz + fzx + gx + hy + iz + j = 0 \quad \text{(C.1)}$$

The coefficients are obtained by minimizing the following equation:

$$L^2 = \sum_k F^2(x_k, y_k, z_k) \quad \text{(C.2)}$$

However, directly solving equation C.2 (by letting $L^2 = 0$) will result a solution where all coefficients are zero! To avoid this, an eigenvector technique can be used [30] by introducing a *scatter matrix* of the given N points $p_1, p_2, \ldots, p_N$, where $p_i = (x_i, y_i, z_i)$ for $i = 1, \ldots, N$:

$$S = \sum_{k=1}^{N} v_k v_k^t, \text{where} \quad \text{(C.3)}$$
$$v_k = (x_k^2 \ y_k^2 \ z_k^2 \ x_k y_k \ y_k z_k \ z_k x_k \ x_k \ y_k \ z_k \ 1)^t$$

The best quadric surface is therefore characterized by the unit vector A that minimizes

$$A^t S A \quad \text{(C.4)}$$

and it is minimized by taking A to be the eigenvector of S associated with the smallest eigenvalue.

Bibliography

[1] G. J. Agin, "Representation and Description of Curved Objects," Ph.D. book, Stanford University, October 1972.

[2] G. J. Agin, "Computer Vision Systems for Industrial Inspection and Assembly," In *Computer*, Vol. 13, No. 5, May 1980, pp. 11–20.

[3] H. Asada and M. Brady, "The Curvature Primal Sketch," In *IEEE Transactions on Pattern Analysis and Machine Intelligence*, Vol. 8, No. 1, 1986, pp. 2–14.

[4] N. Ayache, "A Model-Based Vision System to Identify and Locate Partially Visible Industrial Parts," In *Proceedings of the IEEE Computer Vision and Pattern Recognition*, Washington, D. C., 1983, pp. 492–494.

[5] R. Bajcsy and F. Solina, "Three Dimensional Object Representation Revisited," In *First International Conference on Computer Vision*, London, June 1987, pp. 231–240.

[6] D. H. Ballard and C. M. Brown, *Computer Vision*, Prentice-Hall, Inc., Englewood Cliffs, New Jersey, 1982.

[7] J. L. Bentley, "Multidimensional Search Trees Used for Associative Searching," In *Communications of the ACM*, Vol. 18, No. 9, September 1975, pp. 509–517.

[8] P. J. Besl and R. C. Jain, "Intrinsic and Extrinsic Surface Characteristics," In *Proceedings of the IEEE Computer Vision and Pattern Recognition*, San Francisco, California, June 9–13, 1985, pp. 226–233.

[9] P. J. Besl and R. C. Jain, "Three-Dimensional Object Recognition," In *ACM Computing Surveys*, Vol. 17, No. 1, March 1985, pp. 75–145.

[10] P. J. Besl and R. C. Jain, "Segmentation Through Symbolic Surface Descriptions," In *Proceedings of the IEEE Computer Vision and Pattern Recognition*, Miami Beach, Florida, June 22–26, 1986, pp. 77–85.

[11] P. J. Besl and R. C. Jain, "Invariant Surface Characteristics for 3D Object Recognition in Range Images," In *Computer Vision, Graphics, and Image Processing*, Vol. 33, 1986, pp. 33–80.

[12] P. J. Besl and R. C. Jain, "Segmentation Through Variable-Order Surface Fitting," In *IEEE Transactions on Pattern Analysis and Machine Intelligence*, Vol. 10, No. 2, March 1988, pp. 167–192.

[13] B. Bhanu, "Representation and Shape Matching of 3-D Objects," In *IEEE Transactions on Pattern Analysis and Machine Intelligence*, Vol. 6, No. 3, May 1984, pp. 340–350.

[14] T. O. Binford, "Visual Perception by Computer," In *IEEE Conference on Systems and Controls*, December 1971.

[15] H. Blum, "A Transformation for Extracting New Descriptions of Shape," In *Symposium on Models for Perception of Speech and Visual Form*, W. Wathen-Dunn (ed.), MIT Press, Cambridge, Massachusetts, 1967, pp. 362–380.

[16] J. D. Boissonnat and O. D. Faugeras, "Triangulation of 3-D Objects," In *Proceedings of the 7th International Joint Conference on Artificial Intelligence*, Vancouver, B.C., Canada, August 24–28, 1981, pp. 658–660.

[17] R. C. Bolles and R. A. Cain, "Recognizing and Locating Partially Visible Objects: The Local Feature-Focus Method," In *International Journal of Robotics Research*, Vol. 1, No. 3, 1982, pp. 637–643.

[18] R. C. Bolles and P. Horaud, "3DPO: A Three-Dimensional Part Orientation System," In *The International Journal of Robotics Research*, Vol. 5, No. 3, Fall 1986, pp. 3–26.

[19] T. E. Boult and A. D. Gross, "On the Recovery of Superellipsoids," In *Proceedings of DARPA Image Understanding Workshop*, Cambridge, Massachusetts, April 6–8, 1988, pp. 1052–1063.

[20] M. Brady, "Computational Approaches to Image Understanding," In *ACM Computing Surveys*, Vol. 14, No. 1, March 1982, pp. 3–71.

[21] M. Brady and H. Asada, "Smoothed Local Symmetries and Their Implementation," In M. Brady and R. P. Paul, editors, *The First International Symposium on Robotics Research*, Massachusetts Institute of Technology Press, Cambridge, Massachusetts, 1984. Also appear as *MIT AI Memo 757*, February, 1984.

[22] M. Brady, "Representing Shape," In *Proceedings of IEEE International Conference on Robotics*, Atlanta, Georgia, 1984, pp. 256–265.

[23] M. Brady, J. Ponce, A. Yuille, and H. Asada, "Describing Surfaces," In H. Hanafusa and H. Inoue, editors, *Proceedings of the 2nd International Symposium on Robotics Research*, Massachusetts Institute of Technology Press, Cambridge, Massachusetts, 1985.

[24] R. A. Brooks, "Goal-Directed Edge Linking and Ribbon Finding," In *Proceedings of DARPA Image Understanding Workshop*, Menlo Park, California, April 1979, pp. 72–76.

[25] R. A. Brooks, "Symbolic Reasoning Among 3-D Models and 2-D Images," In *Artificial Intelligence*, Vol. 17, 1981, pp. 285–348.

[26] R. A. Brooks, "Model-Based Three-Dimensional Interpretations of Two-Dimensional Images," *IEEE Transactions on Pattern Analysis and Machine Intelligence*, Vol. 5, No. 2, March 1983, pp. 140-150.

[27] J. Canny, "A Computational Approach to Edge Detection," In *IEEE Transactions on Pattern Analysis and Machine Intelligence*, Vol. 8, No. 6, November 1986, pp. 679–698.

[28] R. T. Chin and C. R. Dyer, "Model-Based Recognition in Robot Vision," In *ACM Computing Surveys*, Vol. 18, No. 1, March 1986, pp. 67–108.

[29] S. A. Coons, "Surface Patches and B-Spline Curves", In *Computer Aided Geometric Design*, R. E. Barnhill and R. F. Riesenfeld (eds.), Academic Press, New York, 1974.

[30] R. O. Duda and P. E. Hart, *Pattern Classification and Scene Analysis*, John Wiley & Sons, Inc., New York, 1973.

[31] R. O. Duda, D. Nitzan, and P. Barrett, "Use of Range and Reflectance Data to Find Planar Surface Regions," In *IEEE Transactions on Pattern Analysis and Machine Intelligence*, Vol. 1, No. 3, July 1979, pp. 259–271.

[32] T. J. Fan, G. Medioni, and R. Nevatia, "Description of Surfaces from Range Data Using Curvature Properties," In *Proceedings of the IEEE Computer Vision and Pattern Recognition*, Miami Beach, Florida, June 22–26 1986, pp. 86–91.

[33] T. J. Fan, G. Medioni, and R. Nevatia, "Segmented Descriptions of 3-D Surfaces," In *IEEE International Journal of Robotics Automation*, December 1987, pp. 527–538.

[34] T. J. Fan, G. Medioni, and R. Nevatia, "Matching 3-D Objects Using Surface Descriptions", In *Proceedings of IEEE International Conference on Robotics and Automation*, Philadelphia, Pennsylvania, April 24–29, 1988, pp. 1400–1406.

[35] O. D. Faugeras and E. Pauchon, "Measuring the Shape of 3-D Objects", In *Proceedings of IEEE International Conference on Computer Vision and Pattern Recognition*, Washington, D. C., June 19–23, 1983, pp. 1–7.

[36] O. D. Faugeras, M. Hebert, and E. Pauchon, "Segmentation of Range Data into Planar and Quadratic Patches", In *Proceedings of IEEE International Conference on Computer Vision and Pattern Recognition*, Washington, D. C., June 19–23, 1983, pp. 8–13.

[37] O. D. Faugeras and M. Hebert, "The Representation, Recognition, and Locating of 3-D Objects," In *The International Journal of Robotics Research*, Vol. 5, No. 3, Fall 1986, pp. 27–52.

[38] C. Goad, "Special-Purpose Automatic Programming for 3D Model-Based Vision," In *Proceedings of DARPA Image Understanding Workshop*, Arlington, Virginia, June 1983, pp. 94–104.

[39] W. E. L. Grimson and T. Lozano-Pérez, "Model-Based Recognition and Localization from Sparse Range or Tactile Data," In *The International Journal of Robotics Research*, Vol. 3, No. 3, Fall 1984, pp. 3–35.

[40] W. E. L. Grimson and T. Lozano-Pérez, "Localizing Overlapping Parts by Searching the Interpretation Tree," In *IEEE Transactions on Pattern Analysis and Machine Intelligence*, Vol. 9, No. 4, July 1987.

[41] K. T. Gunnarsson, "Optimal Part Localization by Data Base Matching with Sparse Data and Dense Data," Ph.D. book, Mechanical Engineering Department, Carnegie-Mellon University, Pittsburgh, Pennsylvania, April 27, 1987.

[42] Martial Hebert and Jean Ponce, "A new method for segmenting 3-D scenes into primitives," In *International Joint Conference on Pattern Recognition*, 1982, pp. 836–838.

[43] T. C. Henderson, "Efficient 3-D object representations for industrial vision systems," In *IEEE Transactions on Pattern Analysis and Machine Intelligence*, Vol. 5, No. 6, November 1983, pp. 609–617.

[44] P. Horaud and R. C. Bolles, "3DPO's Strategy for Matching Three-Dimensional Objects in Range Data," In *Proceedings of the International Conference on Robotics*, Atlanta, Georgia, March 13-15 1984, pp. 78–85.

[45] B. K. P. Horn, "Extended Gaussian Images," In *Proceedings of the IEEE*, Vol. 72, December 1984, pp. 1656–1678.

[46] B. K. P. Horn and K. Ikeuchi, "The Mechanical Manipulation of Randomly Oriented Parts," In *Science America*, Vol. 251, No. 2, August 1984, pp. 100–111.

[47] A. Huertas and G. Medioni, "Detection of Intensity Changes with Subpixel Accuracy Using Laplacian-Gaussian Masks," In *IEEE Transactions on Pattern Analysis and Machine Intelligence*, Vol 8, No. 5, September 1986, pp. 651–664.

[48] S. Inokuchi, T. Nita, F. Matsuda, and Y. Sakurai, "A Three-Dimensional Edge-Region Operator for Range Pictures," In *Proceedings of the 6th International Joint Conference on Pattern Recognition*, October 1982, pp. 918–920.

[49] K. Ikeuchi, "Recognition of 3-D Objects Using the Extended Gaussian Image," In *Proceedings of the 7th International Joint Conference on Artificial Intelligence*, Vancouver, B.C., Canada, August 24-28, 1981, pp. 595–600.

[50] K. Ikeuchi, "Precompiling a Geometrical Model into and Interpretation Tree for Object Recognition in Bin-picking Tasks," In *Proceedings of DARPA Image Understanding Workshop*, February 1987, pp. 321–339.

[51] C. L. Jackins and S. L. Tanimoto, "Oct-Trees and Their Use in Representing Three-Dimensional Objects," In *Computer Graphics and Image Processing*, Vol. 14, No. 3, November 1980, pp. 249–270.

[52] A. K. Jain and R. Hoffman, "Evidence-Based Recognition of 3D Objects," In *Technical Report MSU-ENGR-86-013*, Department of Computer Science, College of Engineering, Michigan State University, 1986.

[53] J. L. Jezouin, P. Saint-Marc, and G. Medioni, "Building an Accurate Range Finder With Off The Shelf Components," In *Proceedings of IEEE Computer Vision and Pattern Recognition*, Ann Arbor, Michigan, June 5-9, 1988.

[54] T. J. Laffey, R. M. Haralick, and L. T. Watson, "Topographic Classification of Digital Image Intensity Surfaces," In *IEEE Proceedings Workshop on Computer Vision: Representation and Control*, August 1982, pp. 171–177.

[55] D. J. Langridge, "Detection of Discontinuities in the First Derivatives of Surfaces," *Computer Vision, Graphics, and Image Processing*, Vol. 27, September 1984, pp. 291–308.

[56] C. Lin and M.J. Perry, "Shape Description Using Surface Triangularization," *IEEE Proceedings Workshop on Computer Vision: Representation and Control*, August 1982, pp. 38–43.

[57] M. Lipschutz, *Differential Geometry*, McGraw-Hill, 1969.

[58] D. Marr, "The Low-Level Symbolic Representation of Intensity Changes in an Image," In *MIT Artificial Intelligence Laboratory*, Memo No. 325, December 1974.

[59] D. Marr and K. Nishihara, "Representation and Recognition of the Spatial Organization of Three-Dimensional Shapes," In *Proceedings of Royal Society of London*, B200, 1977, pp. 269–294.

[60] G. Medioni and R. Nevatia, "Description of 3-D Surfaces Using Curvature Properties," In *Proceedings of DARPA Image Understanding Workshop*, October 1984, pp. 291–299.

[61] D. I. Milgram and C. M. Bjorklund, "Range Image Processing: Planar Surface Extraction," In *The fifth International Joint Conference on Pattern Recognition*, pp. 912–919, 1980.

[62] A. Mitiche and J. K. Aggarwal, "Detection of Edges Using Range Information," In *IEEE Transactions on Pattern Analysis and Machine Intelligence*, Vol. 5, No. 2, March 1983, pp. 174–178.

[63] L. R. Nackman, "Two-Dimensional Critical Point Configuration Graphs," In *IEEE Transactions on Pattern Analysis and Machine Intelligence*, Vol. 6, No. 4, July 1984, pp. 442–449.

[64] R. Nevatia and T. O. Binford, "Description and Recognition of Complex-Curved Objects," In *Artificial Intelligence*, Vol. 8, 1977, pp. 77–98.

[65] R. Nevatia, *Machine Perception*, Prentice-Hall, Inc., Englewood Cliffs, New Jersey, 1982.

[66] M. Oshima and Y. Shirai, "A Scene Description Method Using Three-Dimensional Information," In *Pattern Recognition*, Vol. 11, 1979, pp. 9–17.

[67] M. Oshima and Y. Shirai, "Object Recognition Using Three-Dimensional Information," In *IEEE Transactions on Pattern Analysis and Machine Intelligence*, Vol. 3, No. 4, July 1983, pp. 353–361.

[68] R. P. Paul, *Robot Manipulators: Mathematics, Programming, and Control*, The MIT Press, Inc., Cambridge, Massachusetts, 1984.

[69] T. Pavlidis, *Algorithms for Graphics and Image Processing*, Computer Science Press, Inc., Rockville, Maryland, 1982.

[70] A. P. Pentland, "Perceptual Organization and the Representation of Natural Form," *Artificial Intelligence*, Vol. 28, 1986, pp. 293–331.

[71] P. Perona and J. Malik, "Scale Space and Edge Detection using Anisotropic Diffusion," In *Proceedings of IEEE Workshop on Computer Vision*, Miami, November 1987, pp. 23–28.

[72] J. Ponce and M. Brady, "Toward a Surface Primal Sketch," In *Proceedings of the IEEE International Conference on Robotics and Automation*, St. Louis, Mo., March 25–28, 1985, pp. 420–425.

[73] J. Ponce, "Straight Homogeneous Generalized Cylinders: Differential Geometry and Uniqueness Results," In *Proceedings of DARPA Image Understanding Workshop*, Cambridge, Massachusetts, April 6–8, 1988, pp. 1064–1073.

[74] K. Rao and R. Nevatia, "Generalized Cone Descriptions From Sparse 3-D Data," In *Proceedings of the IEEE Computer Vision and Pattern Recognition*, Miami Beach, Florida, June 22–26, 1986, pp. 256–263.

[75] K. Rao, R. Nevatia, and G. Medioni, "Issues in Shape Description and An Approach for Working with Sparse Data," In *Proceedings of The AAAI Workshop on Spatial Reasoning and Multi-Sensor Fusion*, Chicago, Illinois, October 1987, pp. 168–177.

[76] K. Rao and R. Nevatia, "Computing Volume Descriptions from Sparse 3-D Data," In *International Journal of Computer Vision*, Vol. 2, No. 1, 1988, pp. 33–50.

[77] K. Rao and R. Nevatia, "Shape Description Using Symmetries," paper in preparation.

[78] K. Rao, G. Medioni, H. Liu, and G. Bekey, "Robot Hand-Eye Coordination: Shape Description and Grasping," In *Proceedings of the IEEE Robotics and Automation*, Philadelphia, Pennsylvania, April 24–29, 1988, pp. 407–412.

[79] A. A. Requicha and H. B. Voelcker, "Solid Modeling: A Historical Summary and Contemporary Assessment," In *IEEE Transactions on Computer Graphics and Application*, Vol. 2, No. 2, March 1982, pp. 9–24.

[80] P. Saint-Marc and G. Medioni, "Adaptive Smoothing for Feature Extraction," In *Proceedings of DARPA Image Understanding Workshop*, Cambridge, Massachusetts, April 1988, pp. 1100–1113.

[81] I. K. Sethi and S. N. Jayaramamurthy, "Surface Classification Using Characteristic Contours," In *Proceedings of Internation Joint Conference on Pattern Recognition*, August 1984, pp. 438–440.

[82] S. A. Shafer, "Shadow Geometry and Occluding Contours of Generalized Cylinders", Ph.D. book, Computer Science Department, Carnegie-Mellon University, Pittsburgh, Pennsylvania, May 26, 1983.

[83] D. R. Smith and T. Kanade, "Autonomous Scene Description with Range Imagery," In *Proceedings of DARPA Image Understanding Workshop*, New Orleans, Louisiana, October 3–4, 1984, pp. 282–290.

[84] *User's Manual for the 100A White Scanning System*, Technical Arts Corporation, Seattle, Washington.

[85] A. P. Witkin, "Scale-space filtering," In *Proceedings of Seventh International Joint Conference on Artificial Intelligence*, Karlsruhe, West Germany, August 1983, pp. 1019–1022.